MASTERING ARTISTIC DESIGN

ILLUSTRATOR 10

Hyun Sook Seo and Sae Nan Chong

Illustrator 10: Mastering Artistic Design

Korean language edition originally published in Korea in 2002 by Youngjin.com, Seoul, Korea. All rights reserved.

This edition published 2002 by Muska & Lipman.

Credits: Senior Editor, Mark Garvey; Production Editor, Rodney A. Wilson; Technical Editor, David Karlins; Cover Design and Interior Design and Layout, Chad Planner, Pop Design Works.

Publisher: Andy Shafran

Library of Congress Catalog Number: 2002107565

ISBN 1-929685-76-9

5 4 3 2 1

Muska & Lipman Publishing
2645 Erie Avenue, Suite 41
Cincinnati, Ohio 45208

www.muskalipman.com

publisher@muskalipman.com

Illustrator 10: Mastering Artistic Design

Writer: Hyun Sook Seo
Design Techwriter / Illustrator specialist
Current project head of HOW Graphic at Howcom Publications
Author of: *Illustrator 9*

The leading drawing program among computer graphic programs, Illustrator, is one of the first programs you will come across as you begin your study of computer graphics. In particular, because Illustrator allows you to draw detailed images, it will give you confidence as a designer and it will be your greatest asset in bringing your imagination to life.

The splendid and dynamic features of Illustrator, which allow for liberal editing and detailed graphic work, are great for creating incredibly realistic images. Illustrator surpasses the limitations of other graphic programs and allows designers to fully convey their thoughts and ideas.

Illustrator 10: Mastering Artistic Design is composed of simple examples that take you step by step through using the various editing features to create graphic works. In these projects, you will quickly and easily recreate the various designs, and learn about the great variety of Illustrator's features that you can apply to your everyday work.

As you follow along with the examples in this book, you will learn how to create designs easily using Illustrator, and you'll be taking an important step along the career path of the design professional.

Writer: Sae Nan Chong
Design Techwriter / Photoshop specialist
Current representative in the HOW Design Division of Computer Design at Howcom Publications
Author of: *Creative Photoshop*, *Photoshop 6 Theme Gallery*, *Photoshop Art+ Web Design*

If you want the full light of your individuality and creativity to shine through your work, then Illustrator is the tool of choice.

As the features of Illustrator constantly improve, the realms to which it can be applied also expand. Graphic designers, artists, cross-media design specialists, creative directors, art directors, Web designers, streaming media specialists, Web developers, digital printing specialists, dynamic media specialists—the expanding universe of Illustrator users clearly marks the advent of the era of vector graphics.

But in this Internet era, more than ever, it's important to remember to inject a touch of humanity and emotion in our works.

Project Design: Dong-mi Kim
Design Techwriter / Photoshop specialist
Current project manager of HOW Graphic at Howcom Publications
Author of: *Photoshop Art Gallery, Photoshop 6 Theme Gallery, Photoshop Art Studio*

The step-by-step projects in this book can be followed by anyone. It is a good tutorial for computer techniques from the designer's perspective, and it showcases the skills of a variety of designers.

If you're a beginner, the work you see here may be somewhat daunting—it takes time and practice to understand the subtle correlation between your own knowledge of graphics and computer technology. But by working through the examples in this book, you'll be well on your way to becoming a professional Illustrator designer.

Project Design: Kwang-woo Baek
3D Techwriter / 3ds Max specialist
Current project manager for HOW Design at Howcom Publications
Author of: *3ds Max –The Easy Way, Theme 3ds Max On Your Own, 3ds Max Art & Animation, 3ds Max Art Studio*

The fragments of many thoughts and dreams…
To create a brilliant homepage…
To become an ad designer…
To create your own works of art…

I have put my all into creating a book that reflects the heated (and sometimes cool) passion with which you approach Illustrator. As you flip page by page through this book, I hope that you can feel the various levels of passion within Illustrator.

Illustrator 10: Mastering Artistic Design CD-ROM

The CD-ROM

The CD-ROM included with this book contains all the source images for the examples and all the resultant images seen throughout the book. These images are saved as Illustrator 9 and Illustrator 10 files.

Illustrator 10 Artwork Source Data

All example sources and image files needed are contained in this CD-ROM.

CD/Book_10/

Project 1	1 Source	1 Artwork	10.5MB
Project 2	2 Source	1 Artwork	6.92MB
Project 3	2 Source	2 Artwork	19.9MB
Project 4	4 Source	2 Artwork	34.8MB
Project 5	5 Source	1 Artwork	6.26MB
Project 6	2 Source	1 Artwork	12.5MB
Project 7	1 Source	1 Artwork	1.39MB
Project 8	2 Source	1 Artwork	1.50MB
Project 9	3 Source	1 Artwork	6.07MB
Project 10	3 Source	1 Artwork	31.7MB
Project 11	5 Source	1 Artwork	108MB
Project 12	2 Source	1 Artwork	2.20MB
Project 13	2 Source	1 Artwork	2.27MB

Illustrator 9 Artwork Source Data

All example sources and image files needed are contained in this CD-ROM.

CD/Book_9/

Project 1	1 Source	1 Artwork	10.5MB
Project 2	2 Source	1 Artwork	7.02MB
Project 3	2 Source	2 Artwork	20.3MB
Project 4	4 Source	2 Artwork	34.7MB
Project 5	5 Source	1 Artwork	6.2MB
Project 6	2 Source	1 Artwork	12.5MB
Project 7	1 Source	1 Artwork	1.32MB
Project 8	2 Source	1 Artwork	1.38MB
Project 9	3 Source	1 Artwork	6.34MB
Project 10	3 Source	1 Artwork	31.6MB
Project 11	5 Source	1 Artwork	108MB
Project 12	2 Source	1 Artwork	2.03MB
Project 13	2 Source	1 Artwork	2.05MB

Contents

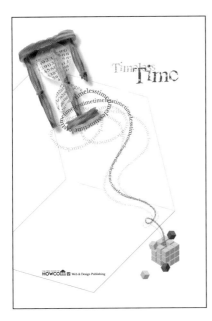

Project 1
Timeless Time 18

Basic drawing tools will be used to draw solid objects, and the Mesh tool will be used to add a sense of realism.
Distortion and alteration features will be used to bring the designs to life and create simple illustrated designs easily and efficiently.

Project 2
Fashion Illustration Design 52

The new Symbol feature of Illustrator10 can be used to create rapidly repeating objects quickly and easily. Reverse rotation, size reconfiguration, scrunch, opacity and color adjustment can all be applied to the symbol tools to attain the desired form quickly and easily. Simple objects, such as leaves, can now be easily made into large groups.

Project 3
Art Flower Design   96

Realistic details are created in Illustrator using the freeform editing feature, Gradient, Mesh Gradient and Blend. The Mesh Gradient tool and Pattern can be used to design even the most detailed images.

Project 4
Design of Editing   128

The text feature of Illustrator not only uses the DTP feature, like word processors and Quark Express, it can also be used for objects. One of the advantages of Illustrator is its ability to recognize entire texts as vector outlines for elaborate and detailed work. The various editing features of Illustrator will be used to create simple, edited designs.

Project 5

Tourism Brochures Design   160

One of the most outstanding features of Illustrator is its ability to easily complete precise and detailed projects. Basic figures are used to design patterns and then these patterns are applied to objects to create images. Illustrator's convenient Edit and Effect features will be used to design a tourism brochure.

Project 6

Tarot Card Design   194

Illustrator, the leading drawing program of all computer graphic programs, is a convenient tool that uses contours for easy drawing and editing. Repeating objects are created easily using Copy, Reflect, Rotate, Shear and alteration tools. Bitmap image filters and the Effect feature will be used to create a unique tarot card design.

Project 7
Time of EGYPT 242

After using the Blend feature to draw the frame of a postage stamp, Illustrator's alteration tool will be used to complete the image of the compass. This simple postage stamp is designed using an Egyptian theme.

Project 8
Wallpainting of EGYPT 270

The upgraded Illustrator 10 offers new and original features that improve the designing process. The dynamic Illustrator tools are used to complete the simple Egyptian postage stamp design.

Project 9
PYRAMIDS   282

Illustrator offers an adjustment feature that is necessary for accurate graphic designing. Illustrator 10, with its new and improved features, allows the user's imagination to take flight. Using the image of a pyramid, the postage stamp design is completed.

Project 10
Ancient Egyptian Museum   294

Illustrator is not only one of the leading drawing programs available, it is also highly compatible with other programs. Text, graphics, images and the diverse Illustrator tools are used to create and transform the postage stamp design.

Project 11
2002 EGYPT Souvenir Stamps 304

Illustrator, like Photoshop, has a Transparency feature that makes use of Blend modes and Opacities to create dynamic effects. The four postage stamps created earlier will be used to design a postcard. The image of the stamps will be arranged and the Effect feature and Shadow effects used to complete the simple postage stamp design.

Project 12
Sensibility of...   318

One of Illustrator 10's improved features, the Liquify tool, will be used to create a design. The Liquify tool conveniently transforms images and design objects and can create everything from the smallest trans-formations to largely exaggerated transformations. Bend and rotate the Liquify tool at will to complete the free-flowing design.

Project 13
City Map Design   318

The Symbol palette will be used to create an old, unique map. Make a symbol and save it in the Symbol palette to easily manage repeating graphics and to reduce the file size. Symbols made in Artwork can also be stored as they are, and original symbols can be edited to automatically update symbols to make Web site management, in particular, more convenient.

Project 1
Timeless Time

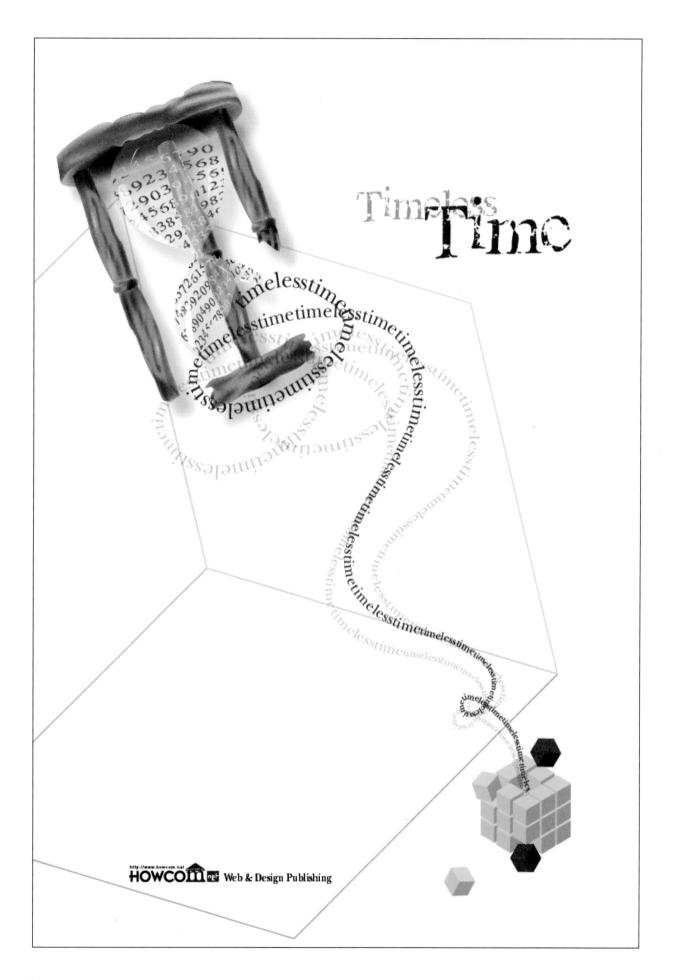

PROJECT 1
Timeless Time

Basic drawing tools will be used to draw solid objects and the Mesh tool will be used to add a sense of realism. Distortion and alteration features will be used to bring the designs to life and create simple illustrated designs easily and efficiently.

Source Files

Logo.eps

ELEMENT 1
Drawing a Hexahedron Using the Shear Tool

Step 1

Open the New Document dialog box by choosing File, New from the menu bar (Command/Ctrl + N). Type "Time" in the Name area of the New Document dialog box, choose A4 from the Size drop-down list, and choose the CMYK Color radio button. Press the OK button to create a new image document.

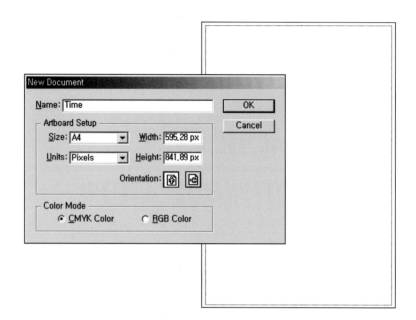

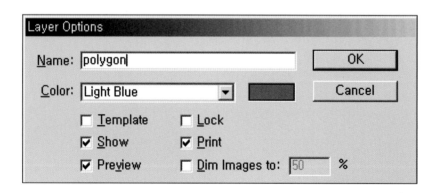

Step 2

Double-click on Layer 1 in the Layers palette to open the Layer Options dialog box. In this dialog box, enter "polygon" in the Name area, and click the OK button.

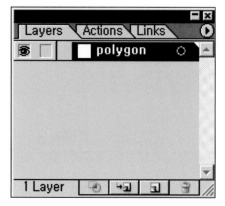

Step 3

Select the Rectangle tool from the toolbox and click and drag to draw a rectangle. Press the Shift key while dragging to draw a perfect square.

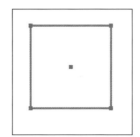

Step 4

Select the Rotate tool from the toolbox and rotate the square so that it is in the shape of a diamond as shown here. Hold down the Shift key to constrain the rotation angle to 45° increments. To flatten the diamond, use the Direct Selection tool and drag the top and bottom anchor points toward the center of the diamond.

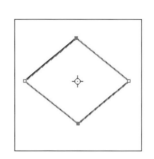
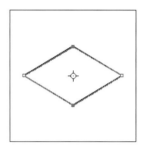

Step 5

Use the Selection tool to select the diamond object. Hold down the Option/Alt key, and drag the diamond so that the second diamond appears as shown here. Use the Direct Selection tool to select the segment at the bottom of the diamond to make a slightly leaning rectangle, as shown here.

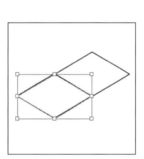
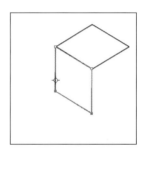

Step 6

Use the Selection tool to select the original diamond. Hold down the Option/Alt key and drag to create another copy of the diamond as shown here. Use the Direct Selection tool to drag on the segment on the right to reshape the diamond so that it fits one segment of the rectangle as shown here. Create the third segment of the rectangle by repeating these steps, as shown here.

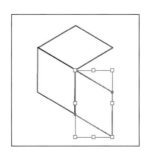
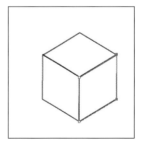
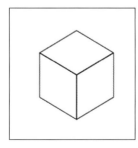

ELEMENT 2
Arranging the Hexahedron in 3D

Step 1

To fill in the hexahedron with color, use the Selection tool to select one segment. In the Color palette, click the Stroke icon to activate it and click None from the CMYK Spectrum. Click the Fill icon to activate it and choose a yellow-green color from the CMYK Spectrum.

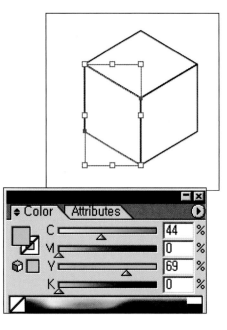

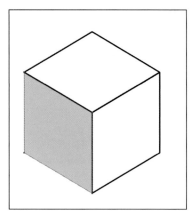

Step 2

Use the Selection tool to select the remaining two segments and fill them using the CMYK Spectrum in the Color palette.

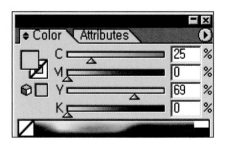

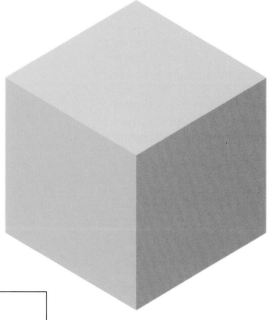

Step 3

Use the Selection tool while holding down the Shift key to select all three segments. To group the three segments, right-click (Command + Click) the selected segments and choose Group from the drop-down menu as shown here.

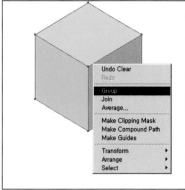

Step 4

Select View, Show Rulers from the menu bar (Command/Ctrl + R). Make guides by clicking and dragging on the ruler. Select the guide with the Selection tool. Using the Rotate tool, move the guide so that it passes diagonally along one of the segments of the hexahedron.

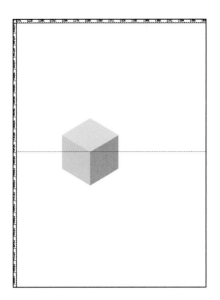
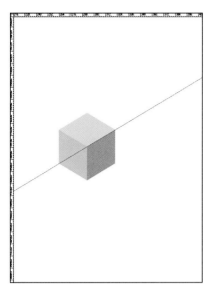

Step 5

Press the Command/Ctrl key, and click and drag on the first hexahedron to create a second, as shown. Select the duplicated hexahedron and right-click (Command + Click). Select Arrange, Send to Back and align the two hexahedrons next to each other along the guide, as shown here.

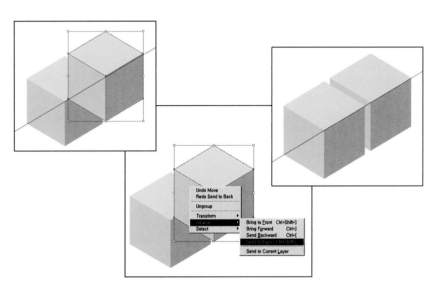

Step 6

Repeat Step 05 and align it along the guide, as shown in the figure.

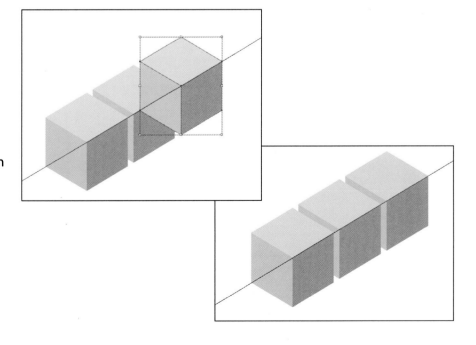

Step 7

To select the three hexahedrons, click and drag the Selection tool over them. Press the Option/Alt key to copy the three hexahedrons below the original.

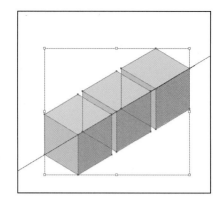
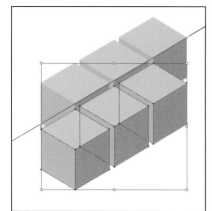

Step 8

With the duplicated hexahedrons selected, right-click (Command + Click) and select Arrange, Send to Back (Command/Ctrl + Shift + [). Stack the two rows of hexahedrons on top of each other, as shown here.

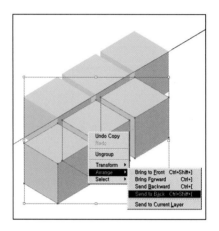
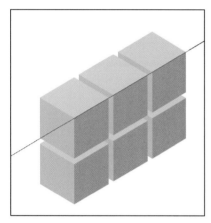

Step 9

We no longer need the guides, so remove them by selecting them with the Selection tool and pressing the Del key. If the top row of hexahedrons is not already grouped, group them by holding down the Shift key and selecting the three hexahedrons. With the row selected, right-click (or Command + Click) and select Group (Command/Ctrl + G). Make a third row of hexahedrons by holding down the Option/Alt key to copy the row below the original. With the duplicated row selected, right-click (Command + Click) and select Arrange, Send to Back (Command/Ctrl + Shift + [). Stack the three rows of hexahedrons, as shown here.

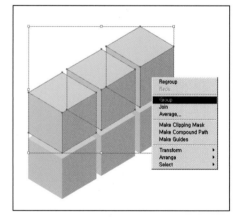
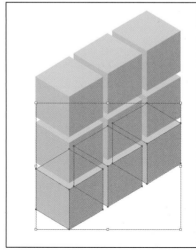
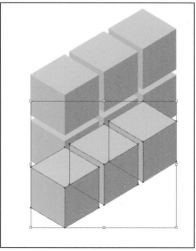

ELEMENT 3
Completing the Hexahedron

Step 1

Select the nine hexahedrons and group them together (Command/Ctrl + G). Click and drag on the ruler at the top of the screen to make a guide. Use the Rotate tool to align the guide against the segment of the hexahedron, as shown here.

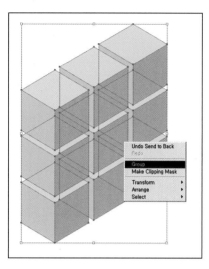

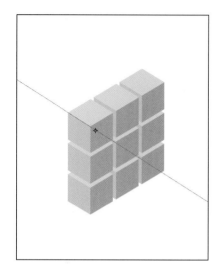

Step 2

While holding down the Option/Alt key, click and drag all the hexahedrons below the original. With the duplicate selected, right-click (Command + Click) and select Arrange, Send to Back (Command/Ctrl + Shift + [).

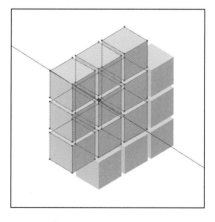

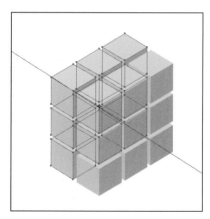

Step 3

Use the same procedure in Step 2 to make the shape of the 3D cube, as shown here.

Step 4

To undo the grouping, select ungroup by right-clicking (Command + Click) on the grouped hexahedron. Use the Selection tool to select one hexahedron and make it into a group.

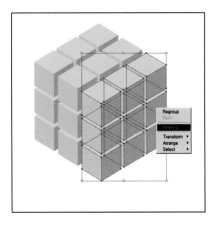

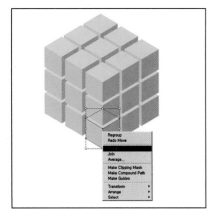

Step 5

Drag the selected hexahedron with the Selection tool and complete it as shown here. Using the Rotate tool, rotate the hexahedron so that it is slightly skewed away from the other aligned objects, as shown here.

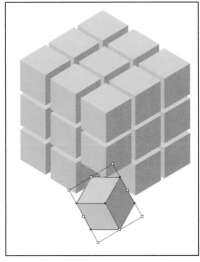

Step 6

Using the Selection tool, group the hexahedron at the top center and drag it as shown here. Use the Rotate tool to rotate the object.

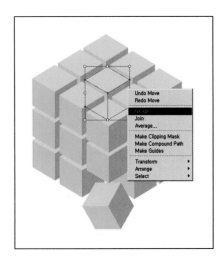

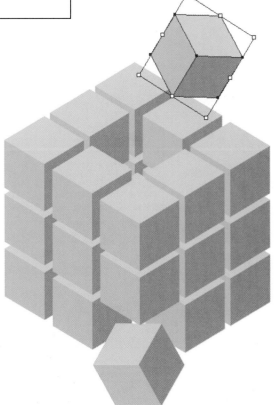

Step 7

Repeat the previous steps to create the image shown here. Select one of the grouped hexahedrons and drag it to the lower left-hand corner, while pressing the Option/Alt key, to make a copy of the object in that corner.

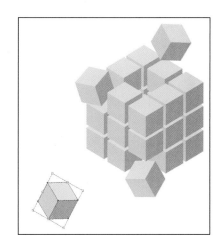

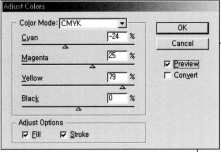

Step 8

To change the color of the objects, select two of the hexahedrons by holding down the Shift key and choose Filter, Colors, Adjust Colors from the menu bar. In the Adjust Colors dialog box, select the Preview checkbox and adjust the color. Click OK when you are done. Fill two hexahedrons with color, as shown here.

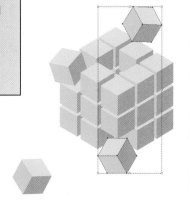

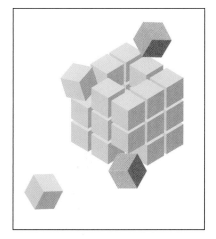

Step 9

From the Menu bar, choose Select, All to select the entire image (Command/Ctrl + A). Use the Scale tool from the toolbox to reduce the size of the image and arrange it in the lower right-hand corner, as shown here.

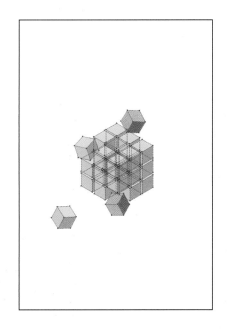

ELEMENT 4
Making the Hourglass Frame 1

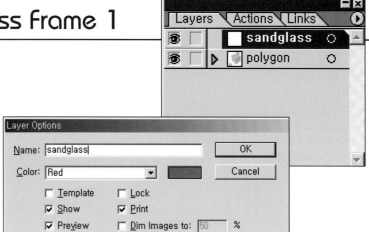

Step 1

At the bottom of the Layers palette, click the Create New Layer button to make a new layer, and then double-click on the new layer. The Layer Options dialog box appears. Type "sandglass" in the Name area and click the OK button.

Step 2

We will now make the wooden frame for the top of the hour-glass. With your image de-selected, in the Color palette, set the Stroke to None and choose a Fill color. When you click and hold down the mouse button on the Rectangle tool, a set of additional tools displays, select the Ellipse tool to draw the elliptical shape at the top left-hand corner, as shown here.

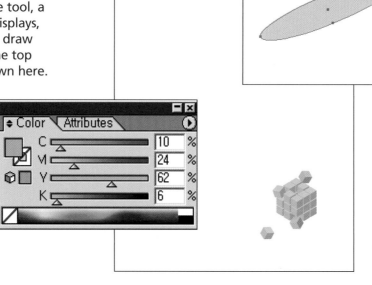

Step 3

Select the elliptical shape and press Command/Ctrl + C to copy it. Choose a Fill color in the Color palette similar to the one shown here, and then press Command/Ctrl + F to paste it with the same center point. Rescale the new ellipse, as shown here.

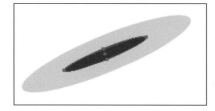

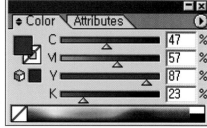

Step 4

Using the Selection tool, select both ellipses. From the menu bar, choose Object, Blend, Make to apply a blend effect (Command/Ctrl + Option/Alt + B).

Step 5

From the toolbox, select the Pen tool and add to the shape, as shown here. Select the Fill in the Color palette and type these CMYK percentages.

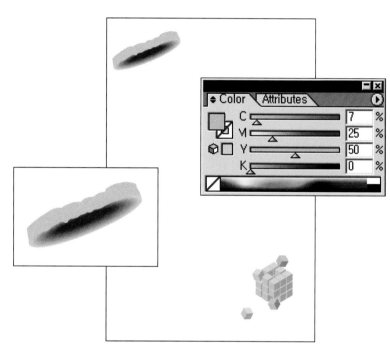

Step 6

From the menu bar, choose Object, Create Gradient Mesh or double-click on the Mesh tool in the toolbox. After configuring the values in the Create Gradient Mesh dialog box as shown here, click the OK button. We can see the configured gradient mesh appear on the object.

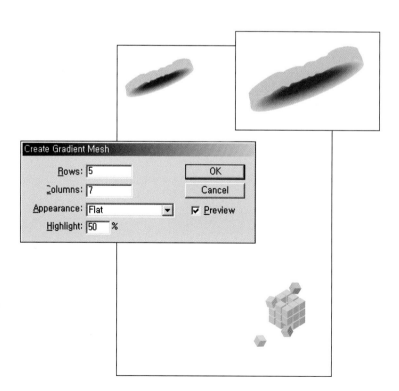

Step 7

Select the Mesh tool from the toolbox and after clicking on the Mesh point, type the CMYK percentages in the Color palette, as shown here. Use the Direct Selection tool to select Mesh anchors. Assign a different color for each mesh point to create a wood grain texture. You can add and remove Mesh lines as needed. To create a new Mesh line, click the plus sign that appears when the mouse passes over the line. To remove a Mesh line, click on the mesh point while pressing the Option/Alt key.

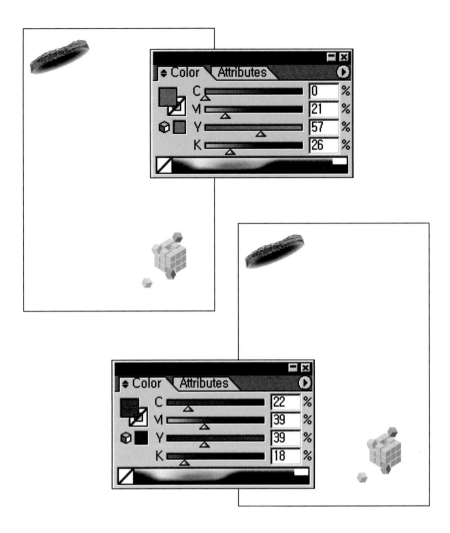

Step 8

Select a color for each mesh point to create a wood grain texture.

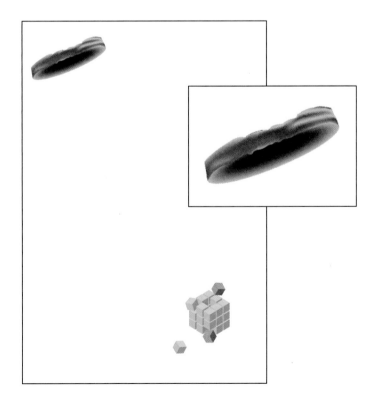

ELEMENT 5
Making the Hourglass Frame 2

Step 1

Select Fill from the Color palette and type the CMYK percentages shown here. Using the Pen tool, draw the hourglass column, as shown here.

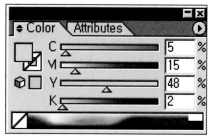

Step 2

From the menu bar, choose Object, Create Gradient Mesh or double-click on the Mesh tool in the toolbox. After configuring the values in the Create Gradient Mesh dialog box with the numbers shown here, click the OK button.

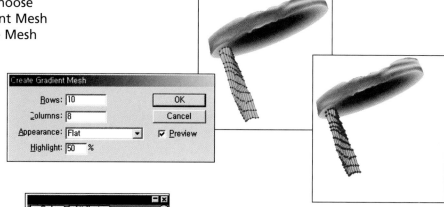

Step 3

Click on the mesh point using the Mesh tool and type the CMYK values in the Color palette as shown here. Select a different color for each mesh point to create a wood grain texture.

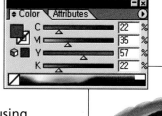
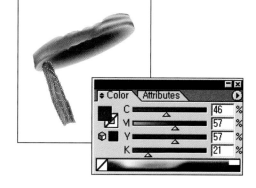

Step 4

When you have finished the color for the hourglass column, you have completed the column.

Step 5

Use the Pen tool to create the additional nub on the bottom of the column. Add a gradient mesh using the Mesh tool, and locate the nub, as shown here.

Step 6

Using the Selection tool, select the column. Right-click the mouse (Command + Click) and select Transform, Reflect.

Step 7

In the Reflect dialog box, choose the Horizontal radio button, and then click the Copy button. You will create a horizontal duplicate of the selection.

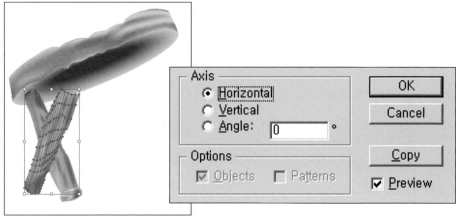

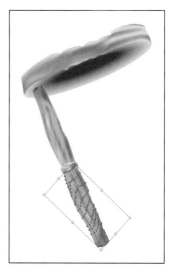

Step 8

Drag down the duplicated selection and rotate it so that it aligns with the existing column. Right-click the mouse (Command + Click) and select Arrange, Send to Back (Command/Ctrl + Shift + [) to connect the two columns.

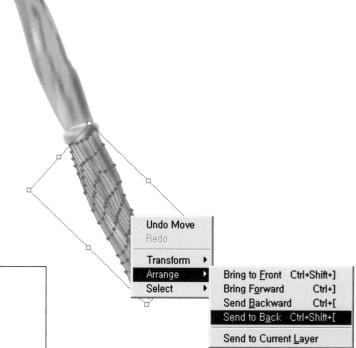

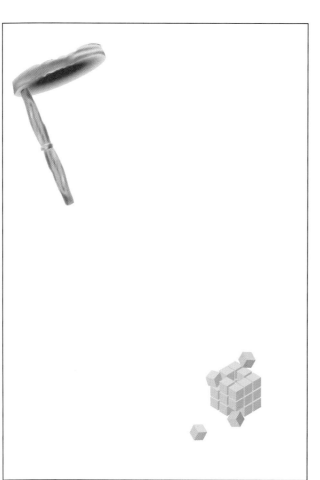

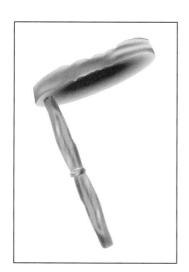

ELEMENT 6
Completing the Hourglass Frame

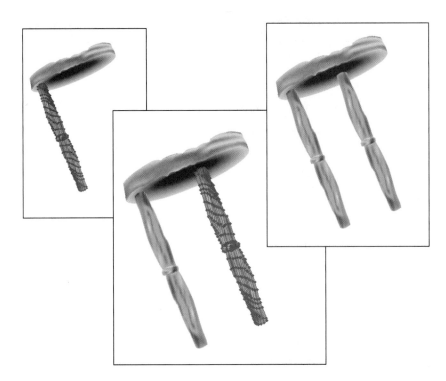

Step 1

Using the Selection tool, select the entire column. While pressing down the Option/Alt key, drag the selection to copy it.

Step 2

Repeat step 1 to select and copy the two individual drawings that complete the column, as shown here.

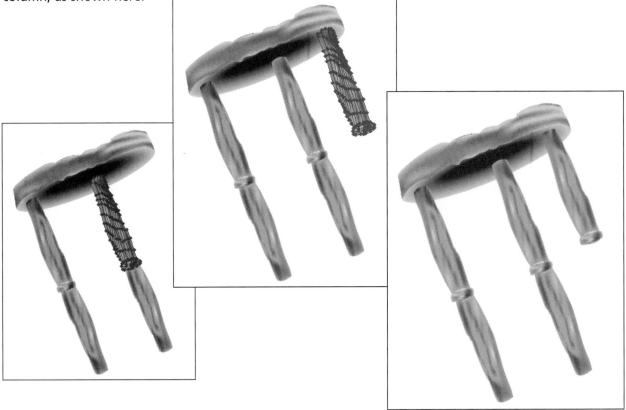

Step 3

Using the Pen tool, draw the image shown here. Using the Mesh tool, complete the image, as shown here. You have now completed the wooden frame for the hourglass.

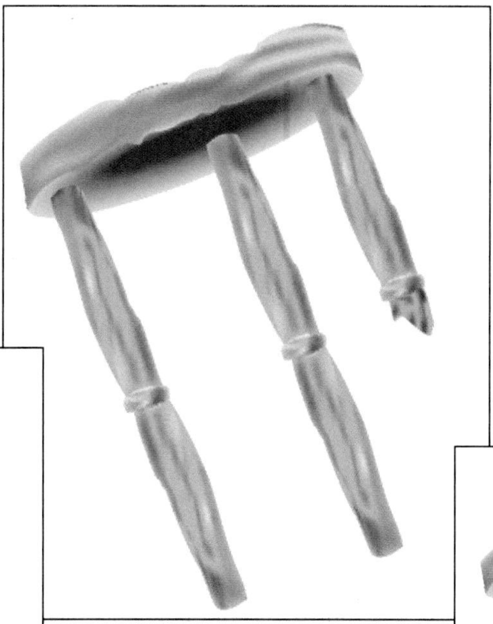

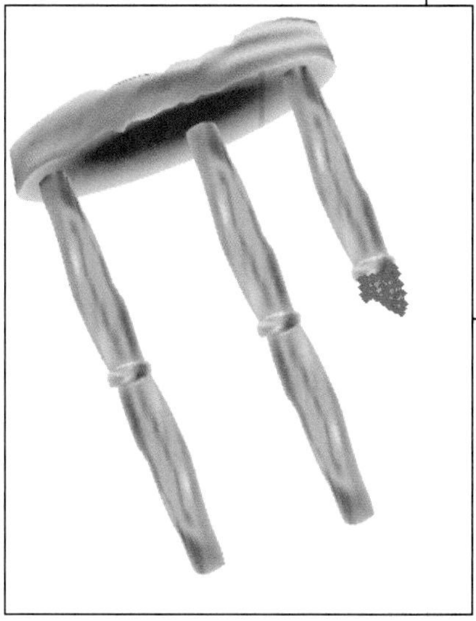

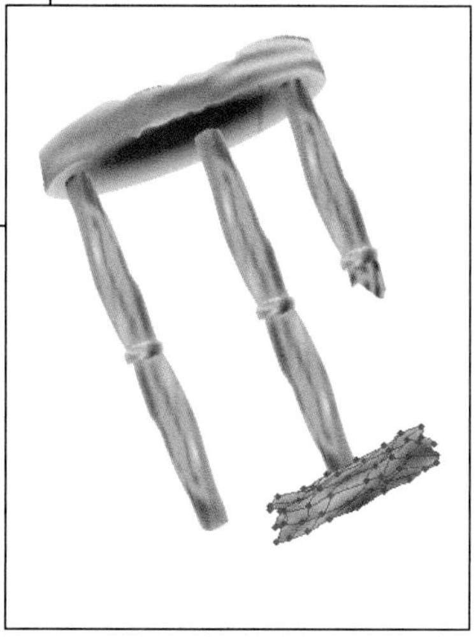

ELEMENT 7
Drawing a Realistic Hourglass

Step 1

Using the Pen tool, draw the shape shown here that will be the hourglass. In the Color palette, set the Stroke to None and select the Fill to the CMYK values shown here.

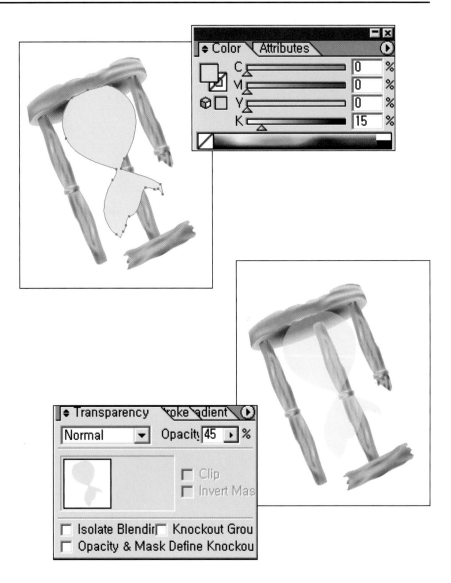

Step 2

Select the hourglass image. In the Transparency palette, set the Blending Mode to Normal and the Opacity to 45%.

Step 3

Using the Pen tool, draw the reflecting light as shown here. In the Color palette, set the Stroke to None and set the Fill to the CMYK values shown here.

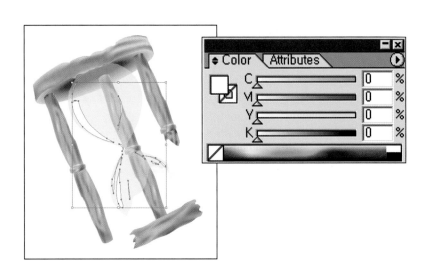

Step 4

To make the reflecting light appear more natural, the edges need to smear a little. To smear the edges, choose Effect, Stylize, Feather from the menu bar. In the Feather dialog box, set the Feather Radius to 2px and click the OK button.

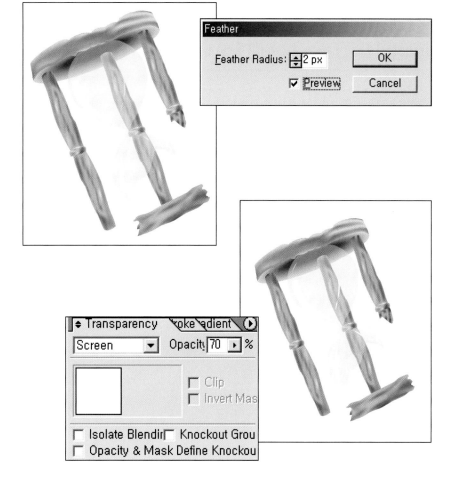

Step 5

To make the light appear more natural, set the Blending Mode to Screen and the Opacity to 70% in the Transparency palette.

Step 6

Use the Selection tool to select the entire hourglass as shown here. Create a shadow effect by choosing Effect, Stylize, Drop Shadow from the menu bar. In the Drop Shadow dialog box, select the Preview check-box and then click OK. You have applied a shadow effect to the hourglass.

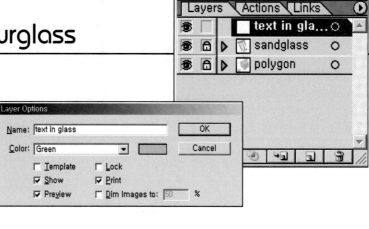

ELEMENT 8
Text Within the Hourglass

Step 1

Click on the Create New Layer button in the Layers palette and double-click on the layer. The Layer Options dialog box appears. In the Name area of the Layer Options dialog box, type "text in glass". Click the OK button. Lock all layers except the text-in-glass layer by clicking in the Toggle Lock box in the Layers palette.

Step 2

To create text for the hourglass, select the Type tool from the toolbox. Open the Character palette by clicking Command/Ctrl + T and select the font, size, alignment and rows. With the Type tool, draw a text box and enter text, as shown here.

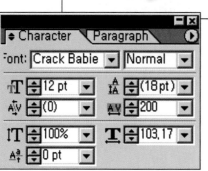

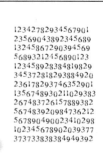

Step 3

Select the text and choose Object, Envelope Distort, Make with Warp from the menu bar (Command/Ctrl + Option/Alt + W). In the Warp Options dialog box, select Shell Upper from the Style drop-down list and adjust the values, as shown here. Select the Preview check-box to see the changes as you make them.

Step 4

In the Layers palette, click the sandglass layer. Select the hourglass and copy it by pressing Command/Ctrl + C. Select the text-in-glass layer in the Layers palette and press Command/Ctrl + V to paste the copied hourglass in the layer.

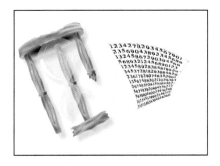

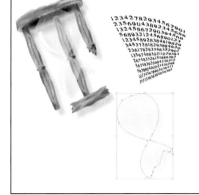

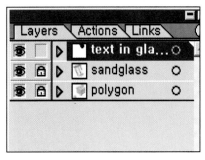

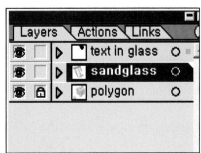

Step 5

To remove the shadow from the hourglass, select the hourglass, and then choose Window, Appearance from the menu bar (Shift + F6). The Appearance palette appears. In the Appearance palette, select Drop Shadow and click the Delete Selected Item button to remove the shadow effect. Then, arrange the hourglass on top of the text, as shown here.

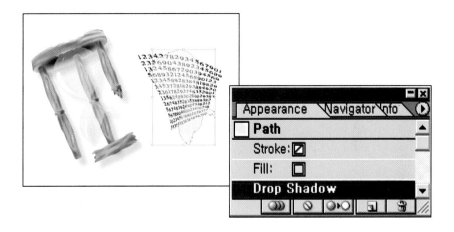

Step 6

Using the Selection tool, select the text and reduce it to fit the size of the hourglass. Then rotate the text so that it aligns in the same direction as the hourglass. Select the hourglass and the text.

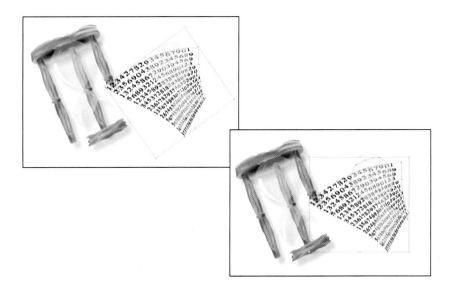

Step 7

With the hourglass and text selected, right-click (Command + Click) and choose Object, Clipping Mask (Command/Ctrl + 7). Make Clipping Mask changes the shape of the text to fit the hourglass. When applying the mask, the mask object must be on top.

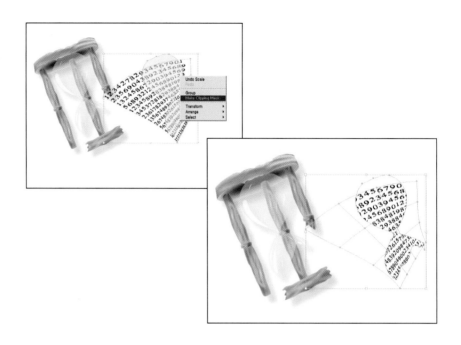

Step 8

Using the Selection tool, move the masked text on top of the hourglass. In the Transparency palette, select Screen from the Blending Mode pull-down list and set the Opacity to 100%. You have completed the addition of the text to the hourglass.

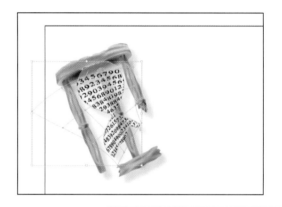

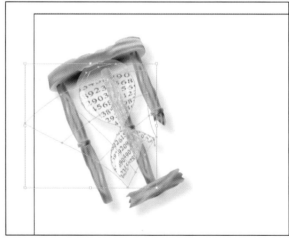

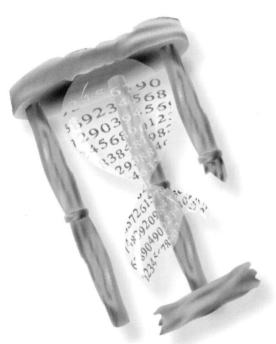

ELEMENT 9
Using the Text to Create freeform Curves

Step 1

Click the Create New Layer button in the Layers palette to make a new layer and then double-click on the layer. The Layer Options dialog box appears. In the Layer Options dialog box, type "text" in the Name area and click the OK button.

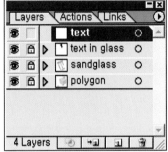

Step 2

We will now make text that follows the line, as shown here. Set the Color to None in the toolbox and use the Pen tool to draw a freeform line.

Step 3

Select the Type tool in the toolbox and specify the font and font size in the Character palette (Command/Ctrl + T). Make the font size gradually smaller to add depth. Type the Fill color for the text in the Color palette, as shown here.

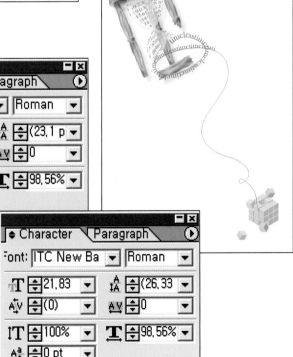

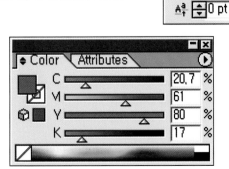

Step 4

Click on the path with the Type tool, type "timeless time," as shown here. In the same way, make the font size gradually smaller to complete the text, as shown here.

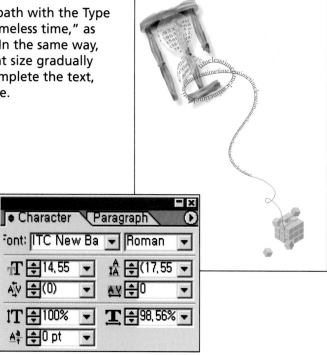

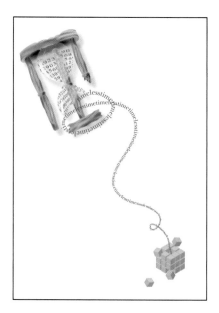

Step 5

Use the Selection tool to select the completed text and drag it while pressing the Option/Alt key to copy it. In the Transparency palette, select Normal from the Blending Mode pull-down list and set the Opacity to 28%.

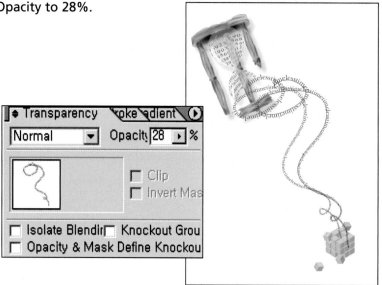

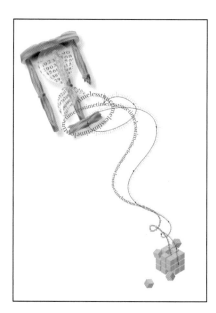

Step 6
Use the Scale and Rotate tools to manipulate the text, as shown here.

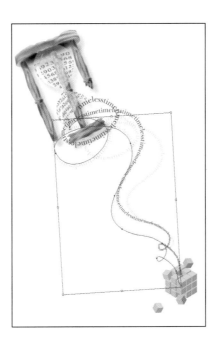

Step 7

Select the Type tool from the toolbox and specify the font and font size in the Character palette. Select the color in the Color palette and type "Timeless."

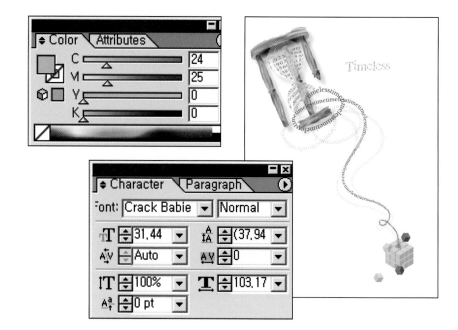

Step 8

Select the Type tool from the toolbox and specify the font and font size in the Character palette. Select the color in the Color palette and enter the word "Time."

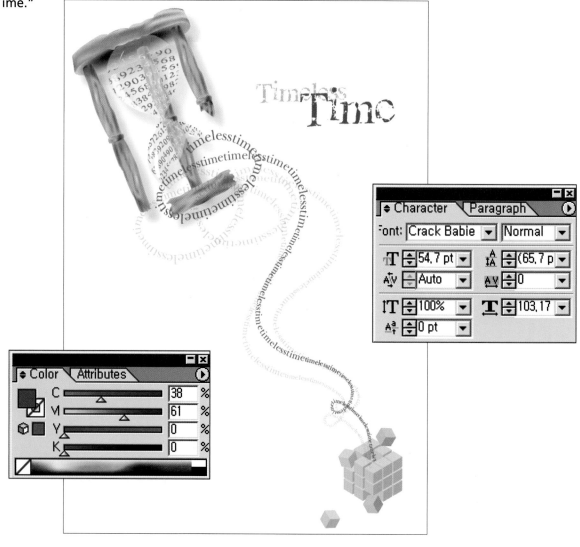

ELEMENT 10
Completing the Logo and Background

Step 1
Choose File, Place from the menu bar to open the Place dialog box. In the Place dialog box, select the Book_10/PROJECT01/SOURCE/LOGO.EPS file from the supplementary CD-ROM and then click the Place button. Then use the Scale tool to reduce the image and arrange it in the lower left-hand corner.

Step 2
Unlock the polygon layer in the Layers palette. Select a hexahedron object and drag it while pressing the Option/Alt key to make a copy.

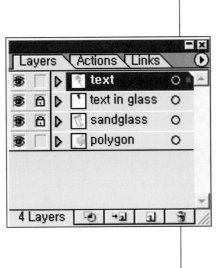

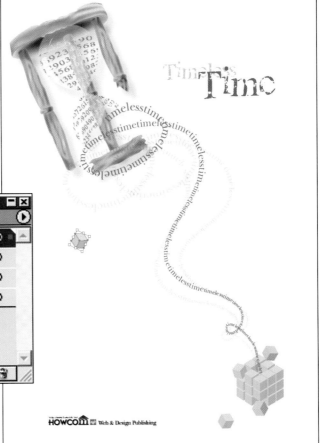

Step 3

Because you will use this hexahedron as the background
image, magnify it as shown
here. Right-click (Command +
Click) and select Ungroup.

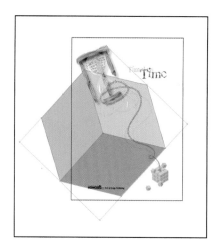
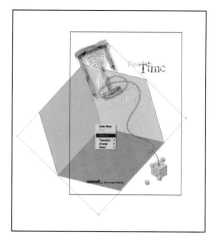

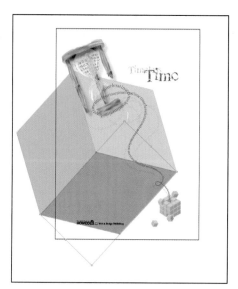

Step 4

Select one of the objects in the
hexahedron and click the Swap
Fill and Stroke button to swap
the Fill and Stroke colors. This
creates a lined object that is
devoid of any color. Select the
object on another side.

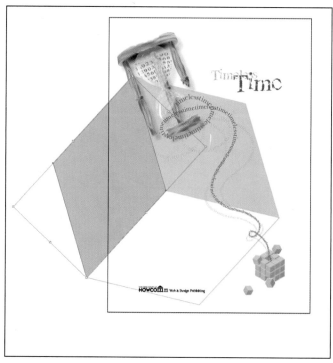

Step 5

Repeat Step 04, click the Swap
Fill and Stroke button to swap
the Fill and Stroke colors.

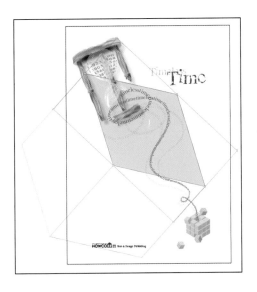

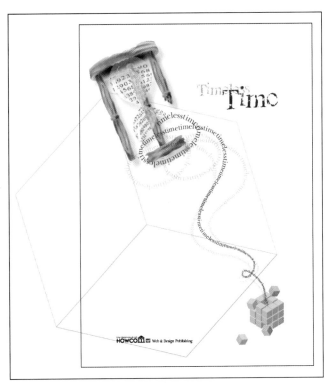

Step 6

Use masks to cover up
unnecessary lines outside the
image. Set the Color to None
in the toolbox and select the
Rectangle tool. Draw an empty
rectangle that fills up the
entire image. Select the lined
hexahedron and the rectangle.

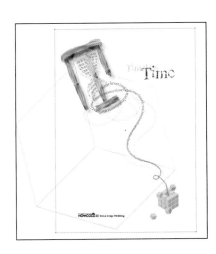

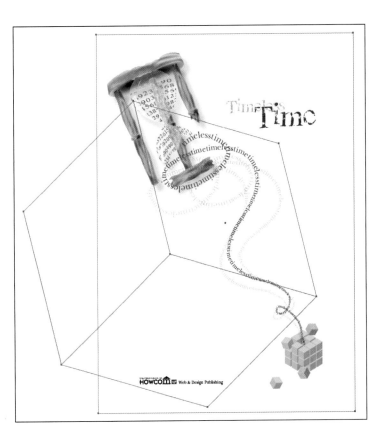

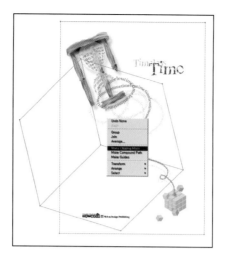

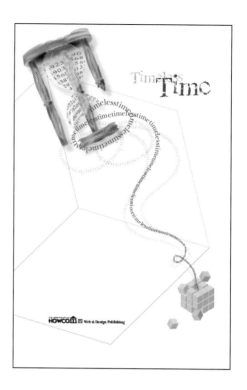

Step 7

Right-click (Command + Click)
and select Make Clipping
Mask. All portions hidden by
the mask are not shown.

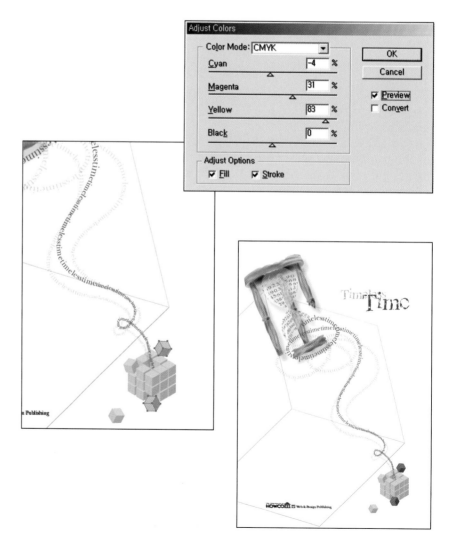

Step 8

To add point colors, select
the yellow hexahedron and
choose Filter, Colors, Adjust
Colors from the menu bar. In
the Adjust Colors dialog box,
select the Preview checkbox
and then click OK.

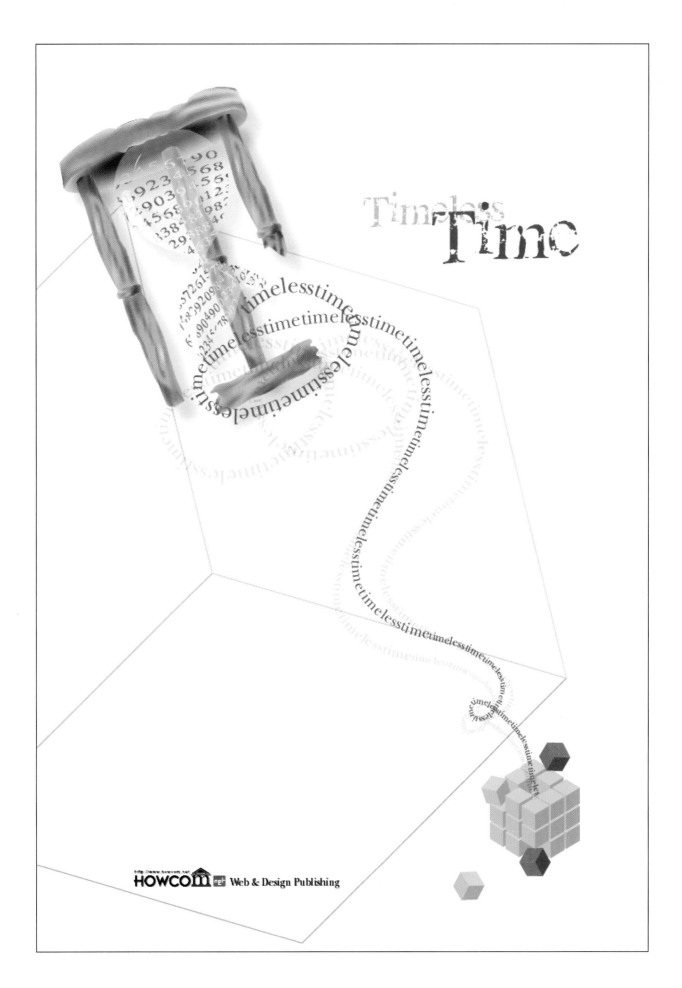

Project 2
Fashion Illustration Design

Opinion
2002 SPRING & SUMMER FASHION ILLUST

Milano Collection is about the return of femininity

PROJECT 2
Fashion Illustration Design

You can use the new Symbol feature of Illustrator 10 to create repeating elements of an image. In the following steps, you will learn how to use the symbol tools to craft an energetic but subtle background. Reverse rotation, size reconfiguration, scrunch, opacity, and color adjustment can all be applied to symbols to create an intriguing image quickly and easily.

Source Files

Drawing.jpg

woman.ai

ELEMENT 1
Creating a Template Using a Rough Sketch

Step 1

Choose File, New to open the New Document dialog box (Command/Ctrl + N). In the Name area of the New Document dialog box, type "fashion illust," select A4 from the Size pull-down list, select Millimeters from the Units pull-down list, and choose the CMYK Color radio button. Press the OK button when you're finished.

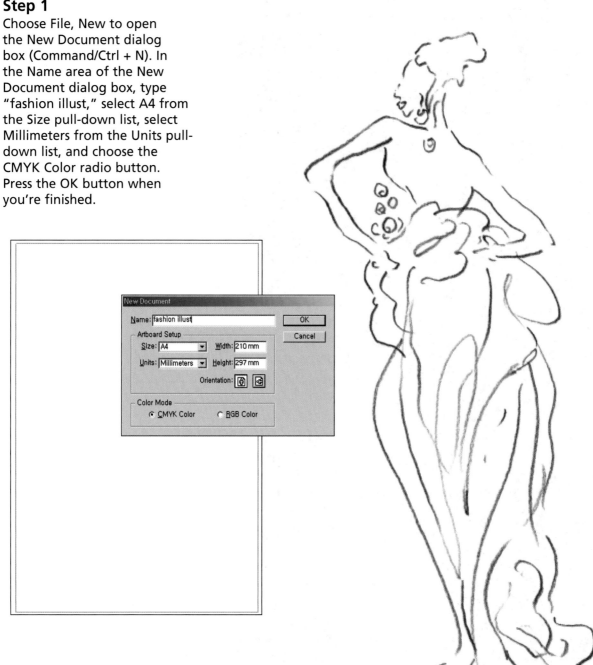

Step 2

Choose File, Place. In the Place dialog box, select the BOOK_10/PROJECT02/SOURCE/DRAWING.JPG file from the supplementary CD-ROM, and then click the Place button to load the DRAWING.JPG image.

Step 3

Double-click the Layer 1 layer to open the Layer Options dialog box. Type "woman" in the Name area and select the Template checkbox. By selecting the Template checkbox, you change the woman layer to a template layer.

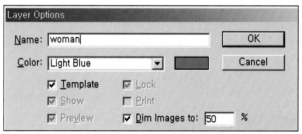

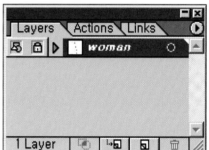

Step 4

You have now fixed the DRAWING.JPG image on the template layer so it cannot be altered by any tool. Fixing the rough sketch on the template layer rather than drawing the image directly using the Pen tool is a much more convenient method and creates a more lifelike image.

ELEMENT 2
Drawing the Overall Line for the Fashion Illustration Image

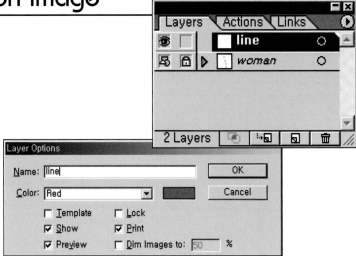

Step 1

Create a new layer in the Layers palette. Double-click the Layer 2 layer and type "line" in the Name area, click the OK button.

Step 2

Set the Fill to None in the Color palette and set the Stroke to black. The Swap Fill and Stroke button flips the configuration. Use the Pen tool to outline the sketch. To see your outline, choose View, Outline so that only the path line of the image is visible (Command/Ctrl + Y).

Step 3

By pressing the Command/Ctrl key while drawing with the Pen tool, you can easily move the point in the direction you want without having to use the Direct Selection tool. The Option/Alt key is a shortcut key for the Convert Anchor Point tool, and clicking the point with this tool will eliminate all direction keys. To draw smooth curves, press down the Option/Alt key again and click and drag to create direction keys on either side of the point.

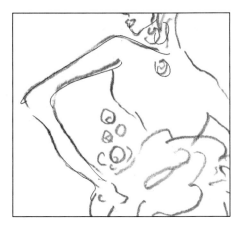

Step 4

Knowing how to use the Pen tool effectively is the secret to creating highly polished elements of art in Illustrator. To add an anchor point to a segment of an existing line, use the Add Anchor Point tool and click the line. To remove unnecessary anchor points, use the Delete Anchor Point tool to click the anchor that you want to remove. Clicking with the Pen tool will create points without direction keys, but clicking and dragging the Pen tool will create points with direction keys. Using the rough sketch as a base, draw the lines one at a time.

Step 5

Zooming in when drawing lines will help you create better detail. To zoom in, either use the Zoom tool or press Command/Ctrl and Space Bar while clicking on the workspace. To zoom back out, press Command/Ctrl, Space Bar, and Option/Alt. The image created using the Pen tool is shown here.

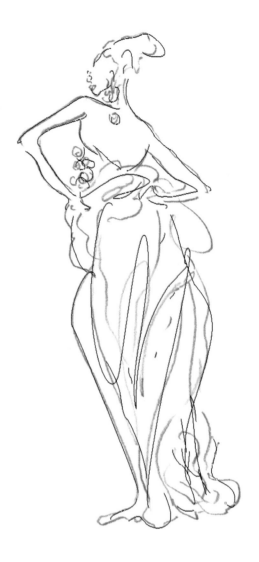

Step 6
Choose View, Preview to
see the black-stroke lines,
as shown here.

ELEMENT 3
Drawing the Body Using the Pen Tool

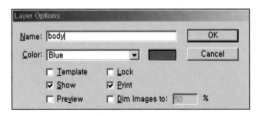

Step 1
Create a new layer in the Layers
palette. Double-click the Layer
3 layer and type "body" in the
Name area, click the OK button.
Lock the line and woman layers
by clicking in the Toggles Lock
box. Lock your layers when
there are many layers or when
images overlap and you want
to affect only one.

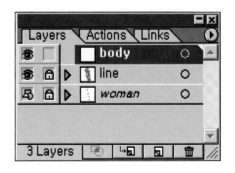

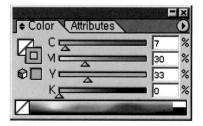

Step 2

Set the Stroke and Fill, as shown here.

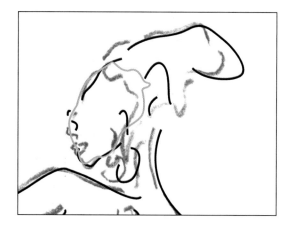

Step 3

Zoom in on the face and draw a closed shape with the Pen tool, as shown here.

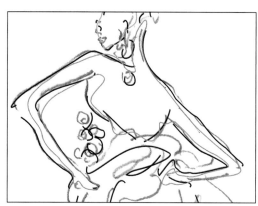

Step 4

Using the Pen tool, outline the torso as you did with the face, as shown here.

Step 5

Use the same procedure to outline the legs, as shown here. You have now completed the basic outline for the body.

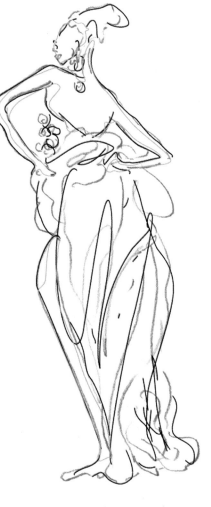

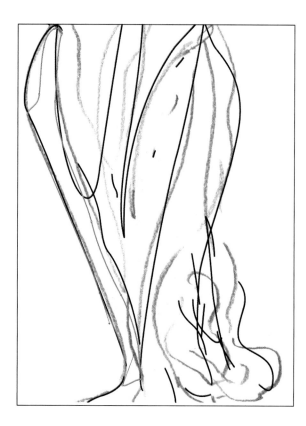

ELEMENT 4
Drawing the Dress Using the Pen Tool

Step 1

Make a new layer in the Layers palette. Double-click the Layer 4 layer and type "dress1" in the Name area, click the OK button. Lock body layer to prevent any changes to it.

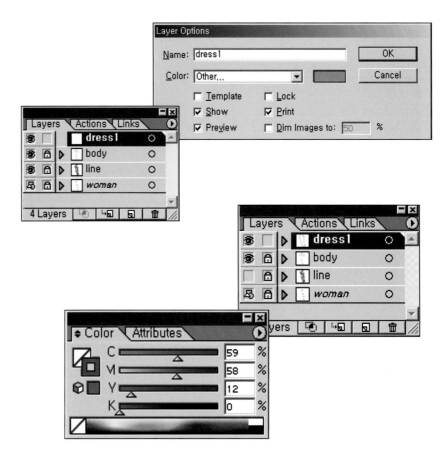

Step 2

Set the Stroke and Fill as shown here. To temporarily hide the lined image, deselect the Toggles Visibility box next to the line layer. Use the Pen tool to outline the dress, as shown here.

Step 3

Create a new layer in the
Layers palette. Double-click the
Layer 5 layer and type "dress2"
in the Name area, click the
OK button. Set the Stroke
and Fill, as shown here.

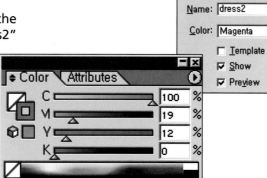

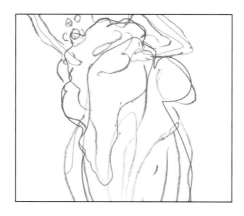

Step 4

To make the dress appear more
natural, use the Pen tool to
draw the folds of the dress.

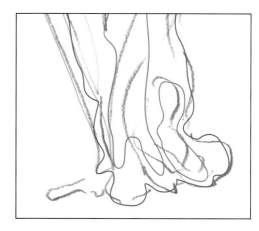

Step 5

As shown here, the
folds of the dress have
been drawn.

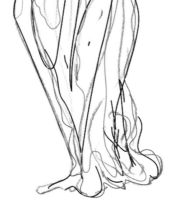

ELEMENT 5
Drawing the Lips and Accessories

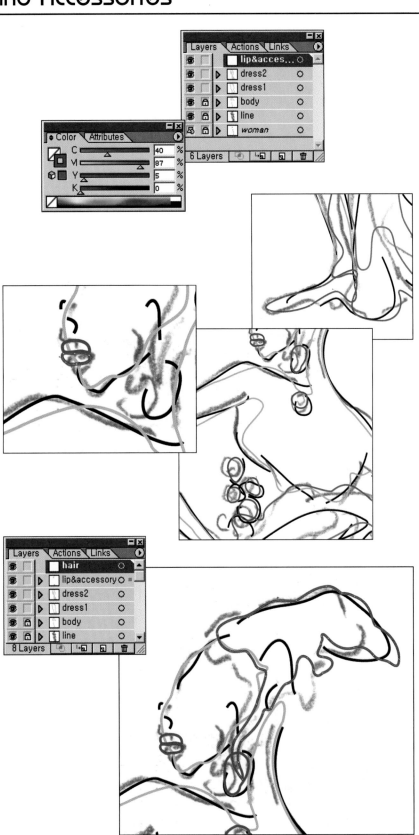

Step 1
Create a new layer in the Layers palette. Double-click the Layer 6 layer and type "lip&accessory" in the Name area, click the OK button. Set the Stroke and Fill, as shown here.

Step 2
Using the Pen tool, draw in the lips, earrings, and shoes, as shown here.

Step 3
Create a new layer in the Layers palette. Double-click the Layer 7 layer and type "hair" in the Name area, click the OK button. Use the Pen tool to draw in the hair, as shown here.

Step 4

Create a new layer in the Layers palette. Double-click the Layer 8 layer and type "hair line" in the Name area, click the OK button. Set the Stroke and Fill, as shown here. Use the Pen tool to draw in the hairline.

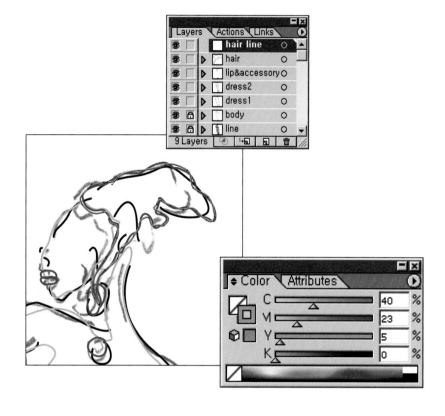

Step 5

In the Layers palette, drag and drop the woman layer onto the Delete Selection icon to remove the template. You have now completed the basic line drawing.

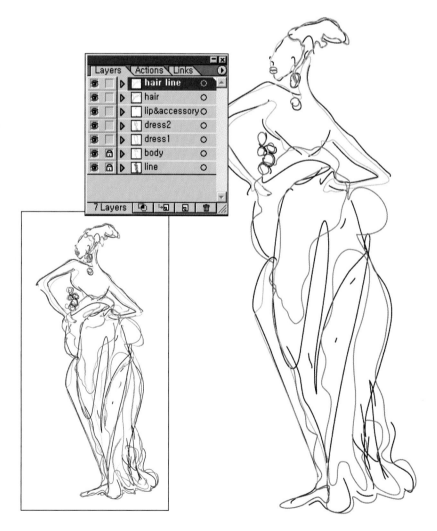

ELEMENT 6
Using the Brushes Palette to Complete the Face

Step 1

Unlock the body layer in the Layers palette. Using the Selection tool, click the face to select it.

Step 2

Select the Gradient tool to create a gradation. Click the left color tab at the bottom of the gradient spectrum in the Gradient palette, which can be found at the bottom of the Color palette. Set the Fill in the Color palette, as shown here. Select Radial from the Type pull-down list in the Gradient palette and click the black color tab.

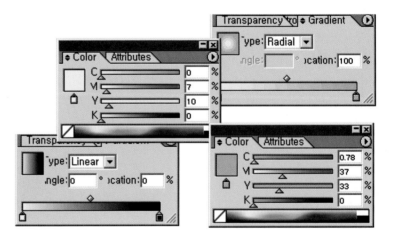

Step 3

Create a natural color for the face, as shown here. Select the Gradient tool. Click and drag from the left side of the face and outwards to create the gradient. Continue this step until the desired result is achieved. To apply vertical or horizontal gradation, click and drag while holding down the Shift key. The longer the distance of the drag, the wider the spread of the color sphere; this creates a more natural result.

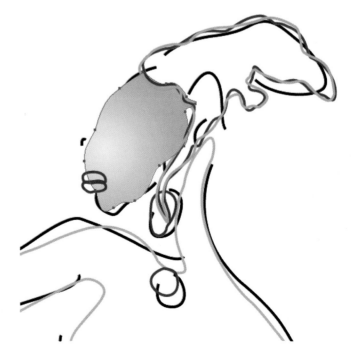

Step 4

Select Stroke in the toolbox and set the color in the Color palette, as shown here.

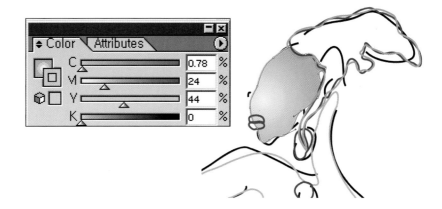

Step 5

Choose Window, Brushes to open the Brushes palette (F5). To load additional brushes into the Brushes palette, choose Window, Brushes Libraries, Other Library. In the Select a library to open dialog box, open Adobe, Illustrator 10, Presets, Brushes folders and double-click the ChalkCharcoalPencil file in the Artistic folder to load the brush file into Illustrator.

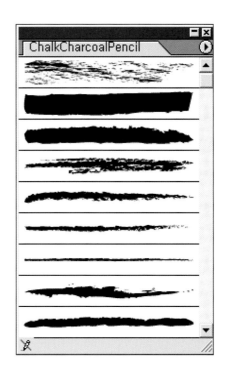

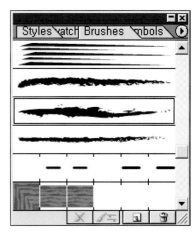

Step 6

Clicking on the brush in the ChalkCharcoalPencil palette will add it to the Brushes palette.

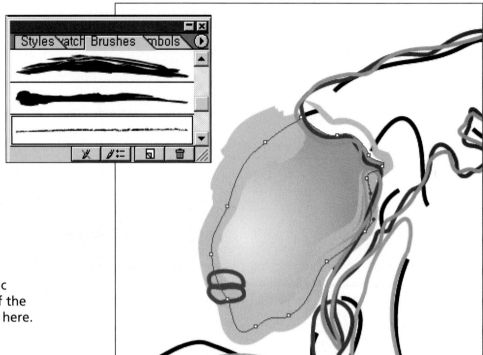

Step 7

Apply one of the Artistic brushes to the stroke of the selected face, as shown here.

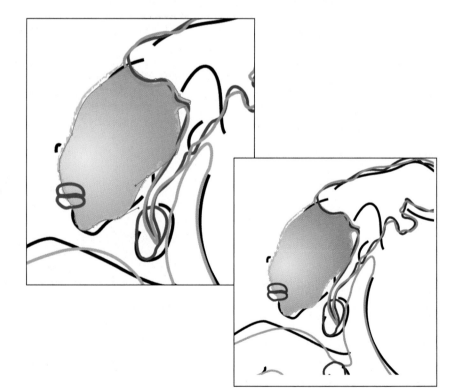

Step 8

Try applying each of the different brushes. Select the desired brush to complete the face.

ELEMENT 7
Drawing the Body Using Gradient and Art Brush

Step 1

Using the Selection tool, select the torso. Using the Eyedropper tool, click the face to apply the same color, gradient, and brush stroke as the face to the torso.

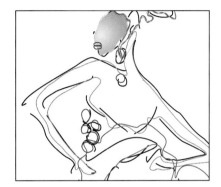 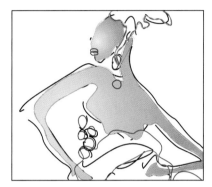

Step 2

Click an empty space below the Gradient Slider in the Gradient palette to create a Color tab. Create a mid-tone color in the Color palette and apply it to the tab. To create a color that is slightly different from that of the face, click the other Color tab in the Gradient palette to switch the colors. Drag the diamond-shaped Location pin in the Gradient palette or drag each of the Color tabs to adjust the color sphere of the gradient.

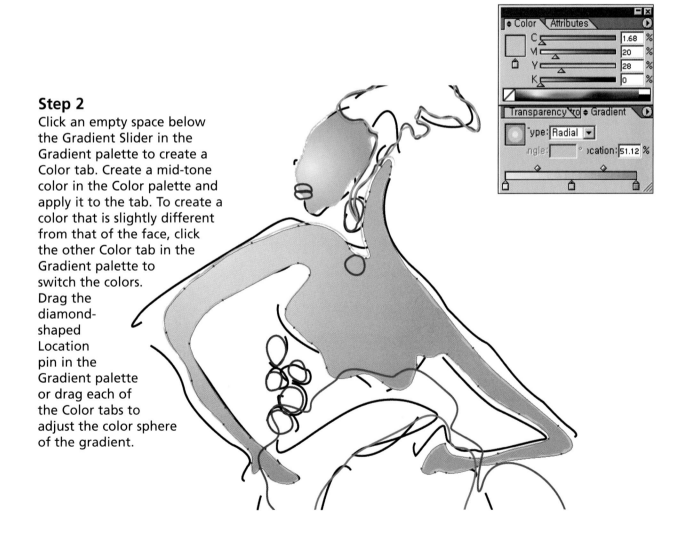

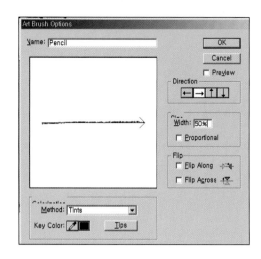

Step 3

To adjust the size of the brush, double-click the Pencil brush in Brushes palette. In the Art Brush Options dialog box, set the Width to 50%, click OK. The Stroke has returned to its original size. Exit from this by clicking on an empty space on the screen.

Step 4

Select the legs by using the Selection tool. Using the Eyedropper tool, click the torso to apply the same color, gradient and brush stroke as the torso to the legs. Continue applying a gradient using the Gradient tool until the desired result is achieved and the color appears natural.

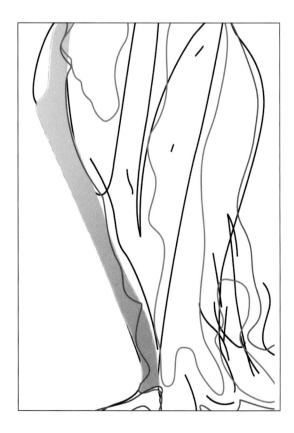

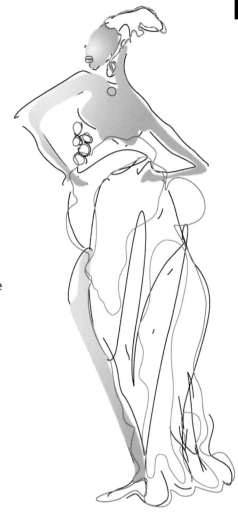

Step 5
You have now completed the body portion of the image

ELEMENT 8
Completing the Dress

Step 1
Select the dress1 image. Click in the empty space below the gradient spectrum in the Gradient palette to create a Color tab. After clicking on the Color tab, select the four different colors that will be applied to the dress in the Color palette.

Step 2

Select the Gradient tool and keep applying the gradient by dragging the mouse until the desired shading is achieved. The gradient will differ depending on the length and direction in which the mouse is dragged.

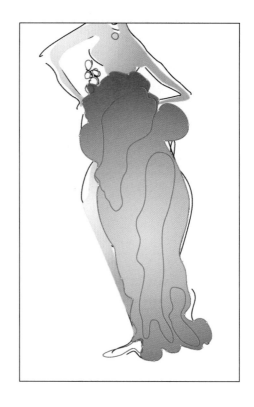

Step 3

Change the Stroke in the Color palette, as shown here. Choose Window, Brush Libraries, Other Library to apply a brush effect to the strokes of the dress. In the Select a library to open dialog box, follow the route leading to the Illustrator 10 program and load the ink.ai file from the Artistic folder. In the Ink palette, click the Dry Ink 1 brush and apply it to the selected object. To decrease the brush size, double-click the Dry Ink 1 brush in the Brushes palette and set the Width to 60%, click OK.

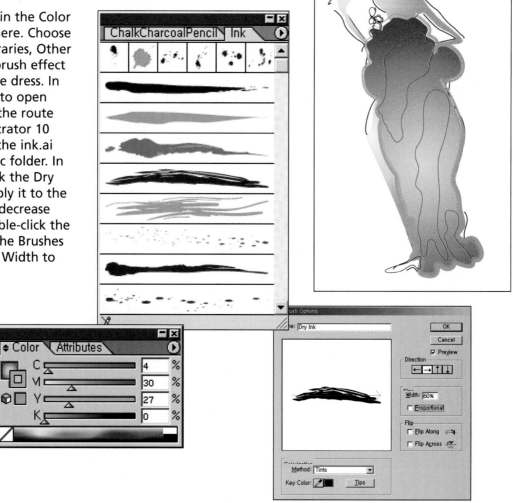

Step 4

Select the first element of dress2. Choose Other Library, and then load the Paintbrush.ai file from the Artistic folder. Click Splash 1 in the Paintbrush palette and apply it to the selected object. Double-click the brush and set the Width to 50%.

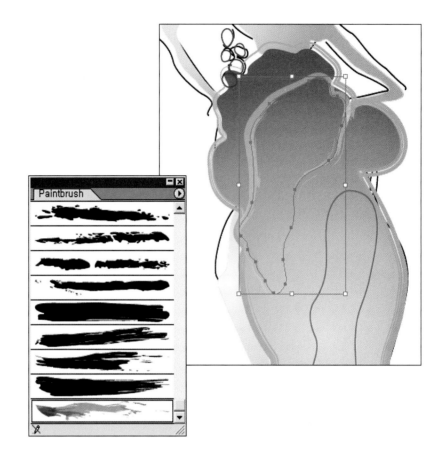

Step 5

Set the Fill color to None and set the Stroke color to a slightly dark pink.

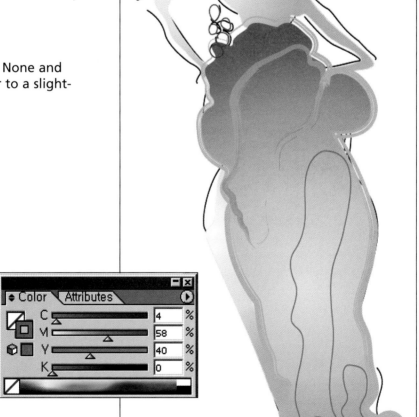

Step 6

Select the second element of dress2. Click the Eyedropper tool on the dress1 image to fill in the Fill color with the gradient color. Select the Gradient tool and keep applying the gradient by dragging the mouse until the desired shading is achieved. Apply the gradient to the third element in the same way.

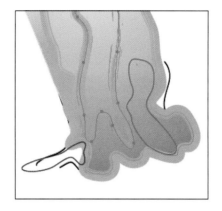
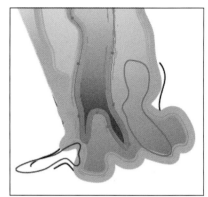

Step 7

Select the shoes. After clicking on the Color tab in the Gradient palette, specify the color value in the Color palette. Unnecessary color tabs can be deleted by dragging them outside of the palette. After specifying the Stroke color in the Color palette, click the Charcoal, Rough brush in the Brushes palette and apply it to the object.

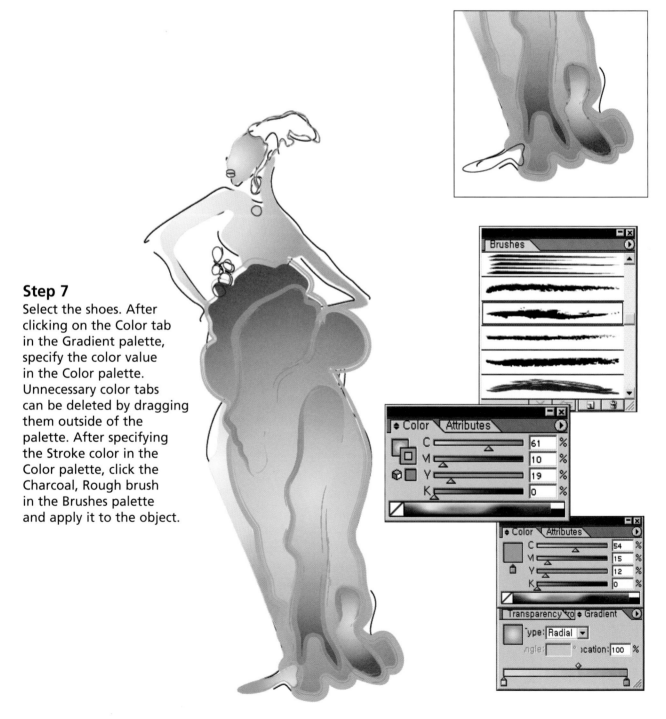

ELEMENT 9
Drawing the Lips, Accessories, and Hair

Step 1

Select the lips. Set the Stroke to None so that only the gradient is visible. After clicking on the Color tab in the Gradient palette, specify the color value in the Color palette. Select the Gradient tool and keep applying the gradient by dragging the mouse until the desired shading is achieved.

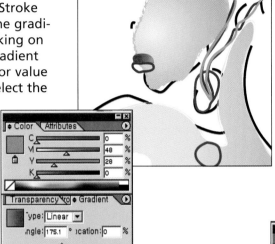

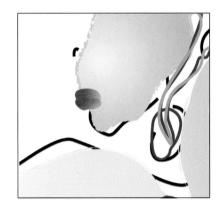

Step 2

Use the Selection tool to select the earrings. Apply a purple gradient as the Fill color for the earrings and apply a brush to the Stroke. Double-click Charcoal in the Brushes palette and set the Width to 10%. Click the Stroke tab to open it and set the Weight to 0.5pt.

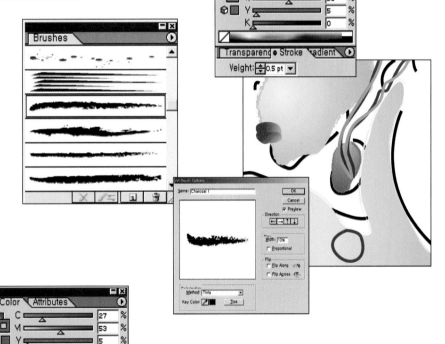

Step 3

Follow the steps above to complete the accessories.

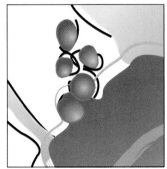

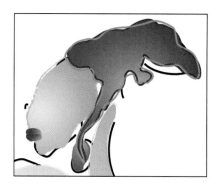 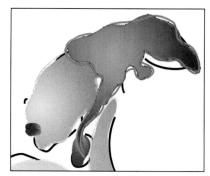

Step 4

Select the hair image. After clicking on the Color tab in the Gradient palette, specify the color value in the Color palette and switch the Stroke color.

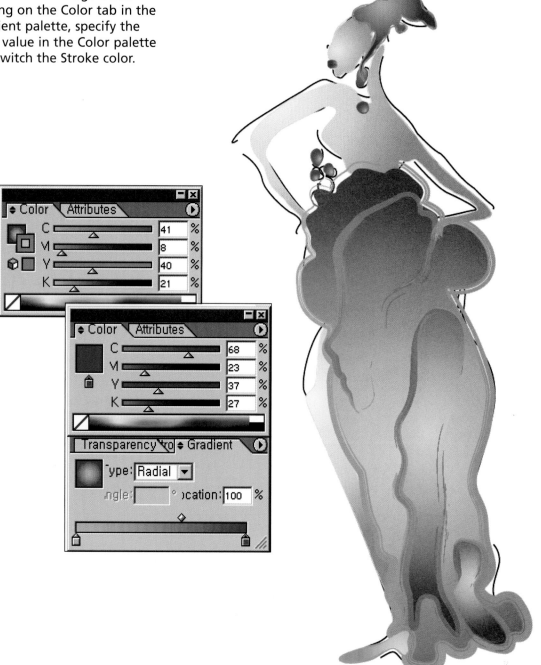

Step 5

Select the hairline image. Double-click the Splash brush in the Brushes palette and then set the Width to 20%. Make it so that only the Stroke color is visible and then set the Stroke Weight to 0.5pt. Exit from this by clicking on an empty space on the screen.

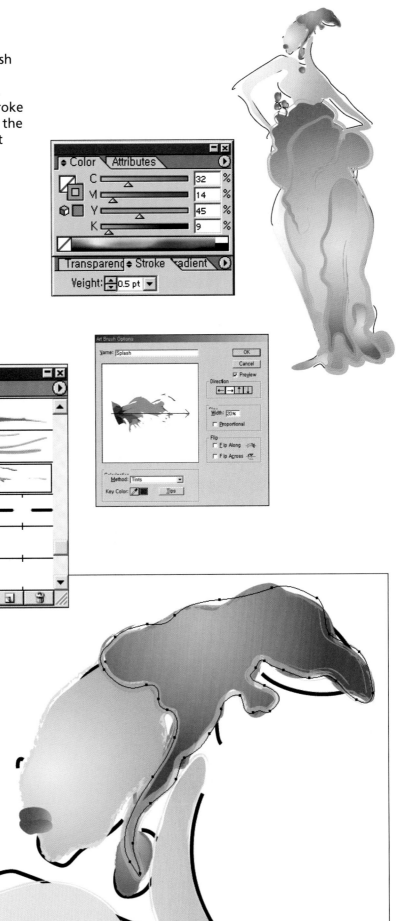

ELEMENT 10
Drawing the Line Using the Art Brush

Step 1

In the Layers palette, drag the line layer to the very top and lock all of the other layers. Use the Direct Selection tool to select the entire image.

Step 2

Choose Object, Arrange, Bring to Front to bring the line image to the top (Command/Ctrl + Shift +]).

Step 3

Click the Fountain Pen brush in the Ink palette and apply it to the selected image. Double-click Fountain Pen and set the Width to 10% in the Art Brush Options dialog box. This will apply the brush to the entire image.

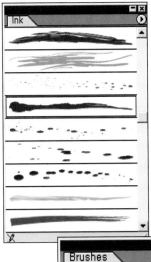

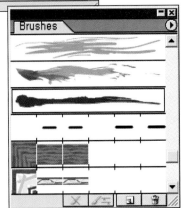

Step 4

The black line of the image is too overpowering. Again, select the entire line image and adjust the color in the Color palette. The image appears much softer, as shown here.

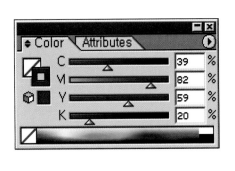

Step 5

Unlock all the layers and then drag the lip & accessory layer below the dress1 layer and select the shoes. Choose Object, Arrange, Send to Back to move the shoes behind the dress (Command/Ctrl + Shift + [).

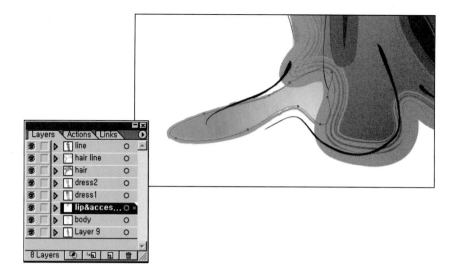

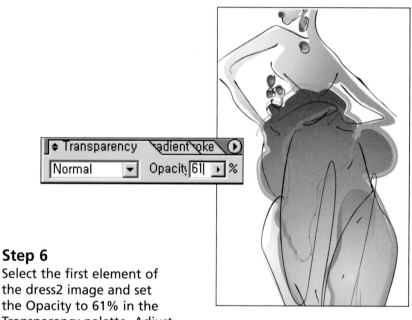

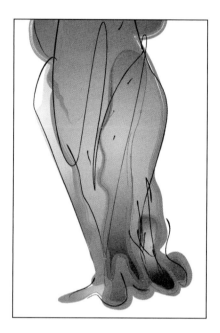

Step 6

Select the first element of the dress2 image and set the Opacity to 61% in the Transparency palette. Adjust the opacities of the second and third elements.

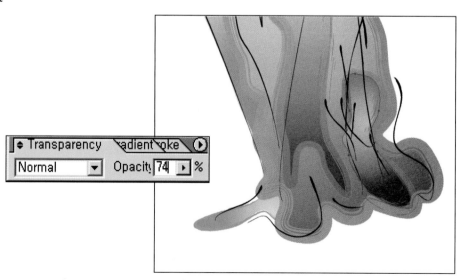

Step 7

Use the Selection tool to select the hairline image and then set the Opacity to 67% in the Transparency palette.

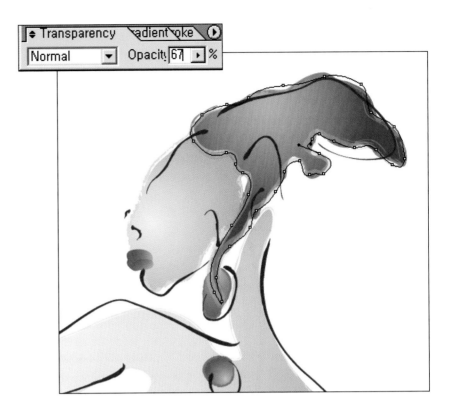

Step 8

To preview the overall image, choose View, Hide Page Tiling to remove the Tiling lines.

ELEMENT 11
Creating the Background Image

Step 1

Create a new layer and move it to the very bottom of the Layers palette. Double-click the layer and name it "background." Select the Rectangle tool and specify the Fill color. Draw the rectangle in the image, as shown here.

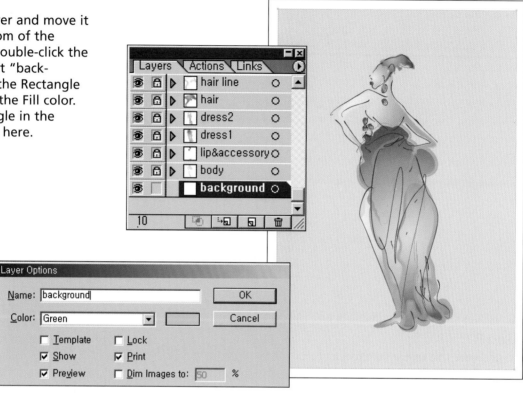

Step 2

In the Transparency palette, set the Opacity to 25%.

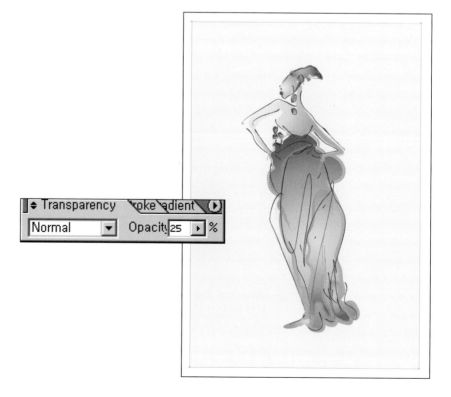

Step 3

Specify the same color for the Stroke and Fill colors. Then, click the Dry Brush 6 brush in the Paintbrush palette and apply it to the Stroke.

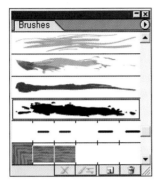

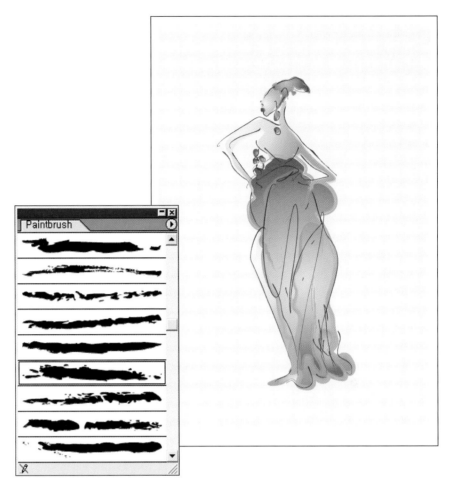

Step 4

Lock the background layer and then select the entire image. Then, move the selected objects to the lower right-hand side of the screen, as shown here.

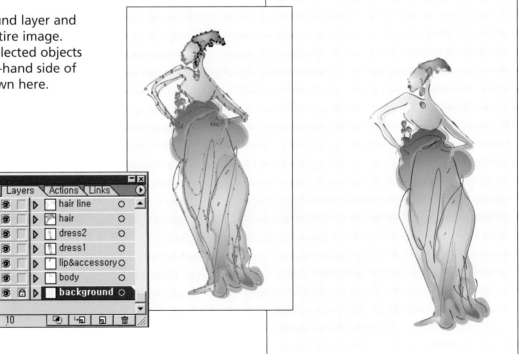

ELEMENT 12
Creating a Simple Title

Step 1

Create a new layer and move it to the very bottom of the Layers palette. Name the layer "title." Select the Type tool and press Command/Ctrl + T to open the Character palette. After specifying the font and font size, type in the word "Opinion."

Step 2

Select the Line Segment tool and specify the Stroke color in the Color palette, as shown here. To make a horizontal line, hold down the Shift key and draw in the line below the text.

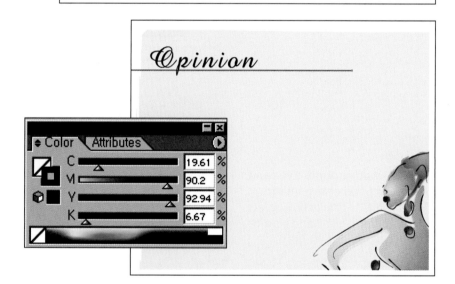

Step 3

Choose Effect, Stylize, Add Arrowheads. In the Add Arrowheads dialog box, set Start to None and End to 21, and then click OK.

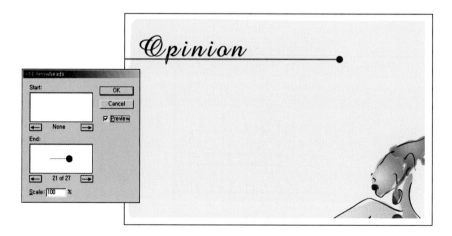

Step 4

Select the Type tool and type, "2002 SPRING & SUMMER FASHION ILLUST."

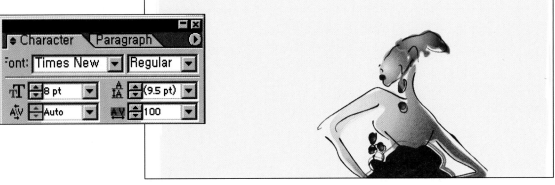

Step 5

Follow the same steps to complete the text written at the bottom of the image, as shown here.

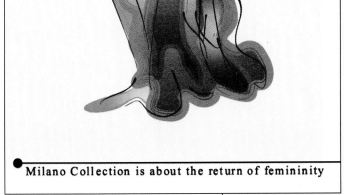

ELEMENT 13
Creating a Spectacular Background
Using the Symbol Feature 1

Step 1

Unlock the background layer
and change the background
color, as shown here.

Step 2

Set the Opacity to 40% in the
Transparency palette.

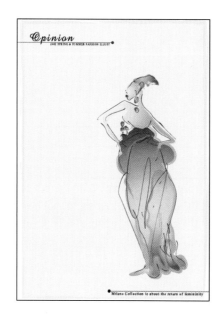

Step 3

Create a new layer and name it "flower." Move the flower layer to the very top of the Layers palette and then lock all the other layers.

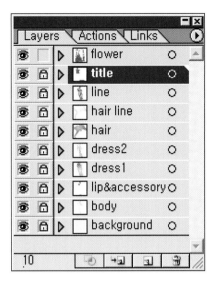

Step 4

Choose Window, Brush Libraries, Other Library and in the Select a library to open dialog box, follow the file folder path leading to the Illustrator 10 program and load the Flowers.ai file from the Floral folder. In the Flowers palette, select the Gardenia brush and drag it onto the image. Note: If you don't have the flower brush installed on your computer, choose another brush.

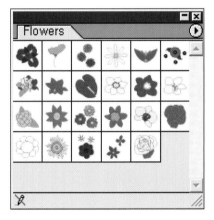

Step 5

Choose Windows, Symbols to open the Symbols palette (Shift + F5). Select the Gardenia brush from the image and drag it onto the Symbols palette to save it as a symbol.

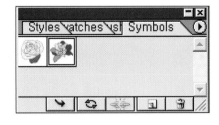

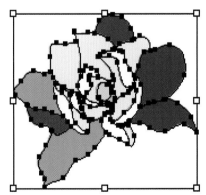

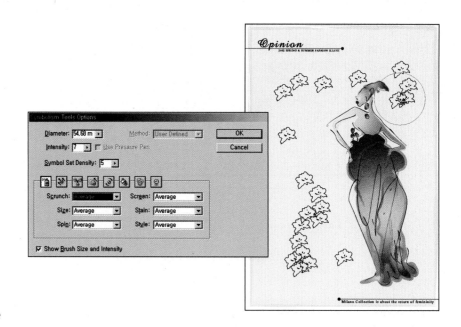

Step 6

In the Symbols palette, select the symbol you will use to fill in the background. Double-clicking on the Symbol Sprayer tool will open the Symbolism Tools Option dialog box. In the Symbolism Tools Option dialog box, configure the properties, as shown here. The mouse cursor will change into a sprayer. Click to spray the symbol throughout the image.

Step 7
Select the Symbol Shifter tool from the toolbox to arrange the symbols evenly throughout the image.

Step 8
Select the Symbol Scruncher tool to create natural spacing between the symbols. Clicking on the symbol will decrease the space between the symbols and clicking on the symbol while pressing the Option/Alt key will increase the space between the symbols.

ELEMENT 14
Creating a Spectacular Background
Using the Symbol Feature 2

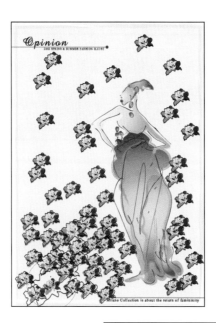

Step 1

There is no rhythm in the image because the symbol objects are the same size. Select the Symbol Sizer tool from the toolbox and click the symbol object to increase the size. Clicking on the symbols while holding down the Option/Alt key will reduce their size.

Step 2

The image also appears slightly awkward because the symbols are facing the same direction. In order to naturally alter the direction of the symbols, select the Symbol Spinner tool from the toolbox. Click and drag on the symbols to change their direction.

Step 3

Specify the Fill color, as shown here. Select the Symbol Stainer tool and double-click it to open the Symbolism Tools Options dialog box. Make the configurations, as shown here.

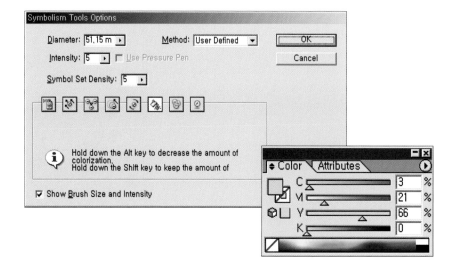

Step 4

It is difficult to create a truly magnificent image using only one color. Use the Symbol Stainer tool to vary the color. A natural gradient will appear where you click.

Step 5

Similar to the previous steps, specify the color in the Color palette, as shown here and use the Symbol Stainer tool to create a gorgeous flower background.

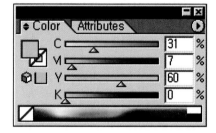

Step 6

You will now add some transparency to emphasize portions of the image. Double-click the Symbol Screener tool to open the Symbolism Tools Options dialog box. Make the configurations shown here and then click OK. Click on the flowers to lighten them.

Step 7

The Symbol Screener tool creates strong and light areas in the image to make the entire image come alive. Clicking on the symbols while holding down the Option/Alt key will make them darker. To create a slowly fading effect, make the symbols in the upper portion of the image lighter.

Step 8

The flowers take away from the main point of the image, which is fashion. In the Layers palette, drag the flower layer to the very bottom to create a soft, yet splendid, background.

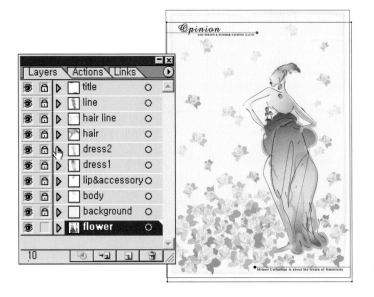

Opinion

2002 SPRING & SUMMER FASHION ILLUST

Milano Collection is about the return of femininity

Project 3
Art Flower Design

PROJECT 3
Art Flower Design

Realistic details are created in Illustrator using freeform editing, gradient meshes, gradients, and blends. The Mesh, Gradient, and Pattern tools can be used to design intricately detailed images.

Source Files

Flower Line.ai

Flower Drawing.jpg

ELEMENT 1
Drawing the Line Using the Pen Tool

Step 1

Open a new document (Command/Ctrl + N). Name the document "salvia splendens," select A4 from the Size drop-down list, Centimeters from the Units drop-down list, and choose the CMYK Color radio button. Click OK. Choose View, Hide Page Tiling to remove the tiling lines from view.

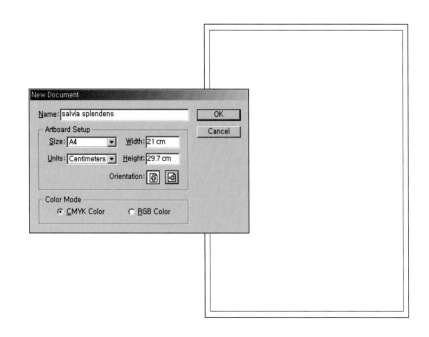

Step 2

Choose File, Place to load the FLOWER_DRAWING.JPG file from the supplementary CD-ROM. Follow this path to find the file: Book_10/PRO-JECT03/SOURCE/FLOWER_DRA WING.JPG file. Double-click the Layer 1 layer in the Layers palette to open the Layer Options dialog box. Rename Layer 1 "template." Select the Template checkbox, click OK.

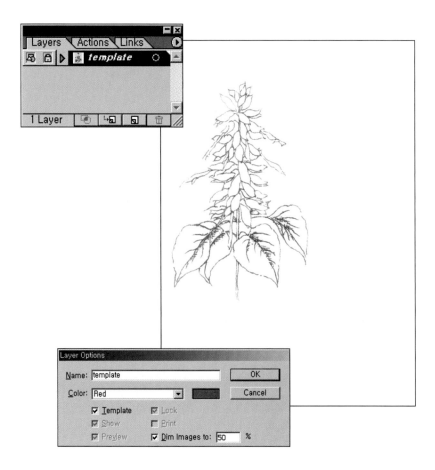

Step 3

Make a new layer and name it "flower."

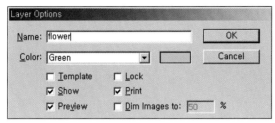

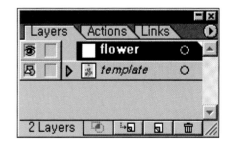

Step 4

Set the Fill to None and the Stroke to black. Select the Pen tool and set the Weight to 0.25pt in the Stroke palette. Outline the flower petals in the template using the Pen tool as shown here.

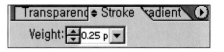

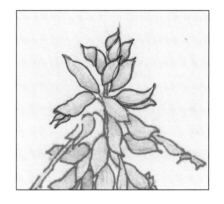

Step 5

Use the Command/Ctrl and Option/Alt keys when using the Pen tool to draw. Zooming in when drawing in the lines is helpful when creating detail. To zoom in, either use the Zoom tool or press Command/Ctrl and Space Bar while clicking. To zoom back out, click while pressing Command/Ctrl, Space Bar, and Option/Alt.

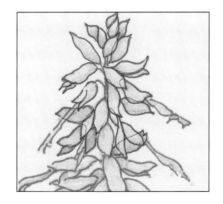

Step 6

Finish outlining the flower petals and then outline the leaves and the stem using the Pen tool.

Step 7

Delete the template layer by dragging and dropping it over the Delete Selection icon in the Layers palette. Select the entire image. Holding down the Option/Alt key, drag the image to the side to make a copy. You'll use this copy later in the project.

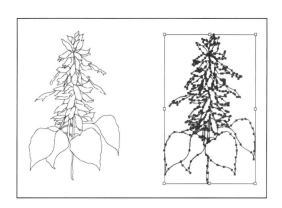

ELEMENT 2
Using the Gradient Mesh Tool

Step 1

Select one of the flower petals using the Direct Selection tool. Set the Fill color in the Color palette as shown here.

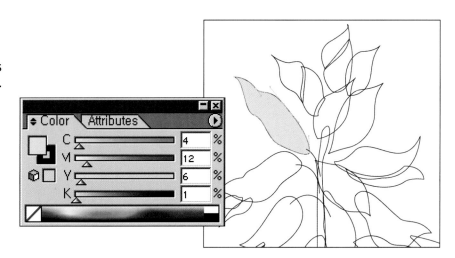

Step 2

Choose Object, Create Gradient Mesh from the menu bar. In the Create Gradient Mesh dialog box, select the Preview checkbox, set the Rows to 3, the Columns to 3, and select Flat from the Appearance drop-down list. A mesh line will appear inside the flower petal.

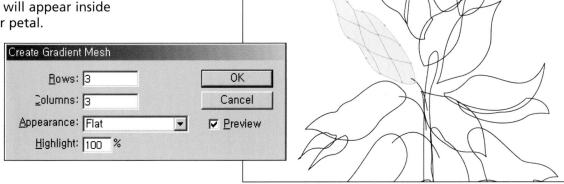

Step 3

Select one of the several mesh points inside the petal using the Direct Selection tool. Select a slightly darker color in the Color palette to create a soft gradient around the selected mesh point, as shown here.

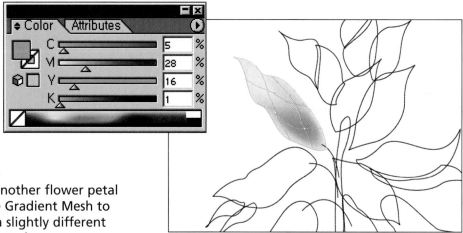

Step 4

Select another flower petal and use Gradient Mesh to create a slightly different flower petal.

ELEMENT 3
Completing the Flower Petal Using the Gradient Mesh Tool

Step 1

Use the Direct Selection tool to select a flower petal as shown here. Choose Object, Create Gradient Mesh. In the Create Gradient Mesh dialog box, select the Preview checkbox, set the Rows to 3, the Columns to 3, and select To Center from the Appearance drop-down list. The center of the petal will appear bright while a mesh line appears inside the selected petal according to your configurations.

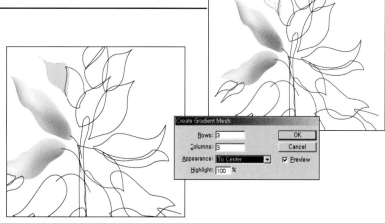

Step 2

Select To Center from the Appearance drop-down list when you want to lighten the inside of an image. Use the same method to apply a gradient mesh to the other flower petals.

Step 3

Right-click (Command + Click) the mouse on the selected petal and Choose Arrange, Send Backward to send the object to the back (Command/Ctrl + [).

Step 4

Use the same method to apply the gradient mesh to the remainder of the petals, as shown here.

ELEMENT 4
Completing the Stem Using the Gradient Mesh and Brush Tools

Step 1

Use the Direct Selection tool to select the stem of the flower, as shown here. Choose Object, Create Gradient Mesh. In the Create Gradient Mesh dialog box, select the Preview checkbox, set the Rows to 10, the Columns to 2, and select Flat from the Appearance drop-down list. A mesh line will appear inside the selected stem.

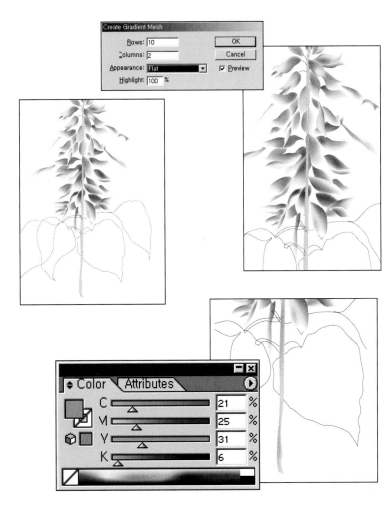

Step 2

Select one of the several mesh points inside the stem using the Direct Selection tool. Select a slightly darker color in the Color palette to create a soft gradient around the selected mesh point.

Step 3

Right-click (Command + Click) the mouse on the stem and Choose Arrange, Send To Back (Command/Ctrl + [).

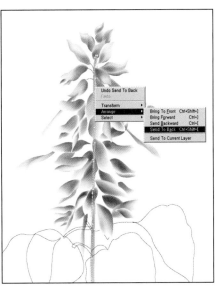

Step 4

Use the Direct Selection tool to select the small petal stems. Select Window, Brushes to open the Brushes palette (F5). To add the Artistic brush to the Brushes palette, choose Window, Brush Libraries, Other Library. In the Select a library to open dialog box, open the Adobe, Illustrator 10, Presets, Brushes, Artistic folders in this order and double-click the Watercolor.ai file to load this brush file. Click the Wet brush in the Watercolor palette to add it to the Brushes palette. Note: If you don't have the Watercolor file loaded on your computer, choose a different Brush.

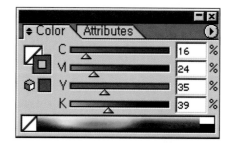

Step 5

Select Stroke in the Color palette and set the color as shown here. To reduce the size of the brush, choose Window, Appearance and, in the Appearances dialog box, double-click Stroke to open the Stroke Options dialog box. In the Stroke dialog box, set the Width to 20% and click OK to apply this new brush size.

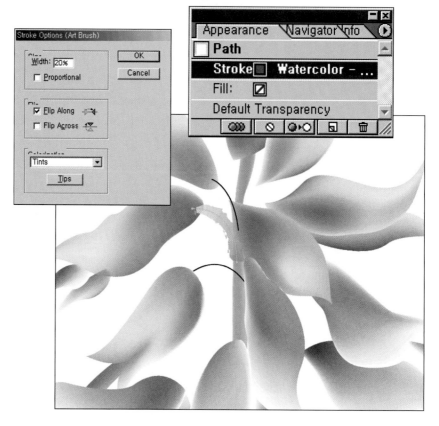

Step 6

Using the Selection tool, select all elements to which you want to apply the brush stroke. To select several elements at the same time, hold down the Shift key while selecting the elements. Clicking the Eyedropper tool on the image to which the brush has already been applied will apply it to the other selected objects. With the stalk objects selected, right-click (Command + Click) the mouse and Choose Arrange, Send to Back (Command/Ctrl + Shift + [).

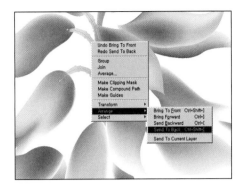

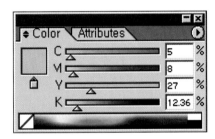

Step 7

Use the Selection tool to select the stem at the bottom of the image. Select Window, Gradient to open the Gradient palette (F9). In the Gradient palette, set the Type to Linear and click on the Color tab. Select the color in the Color palette as shown here.

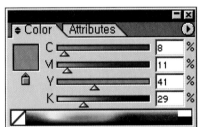

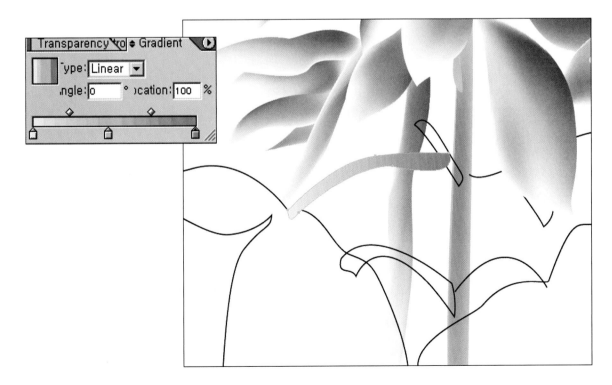

Step 8

Clicking the Eyedropper tool on the stem objects to which the gradient has already been applied will apply it to the other selected objects. Right-click (Command + Click) the mouse and Choose Arrange, Send to Back (Command/Ctrl + Shift + [).

Step 9

Selecting the remaining stem elements, click the Eyedropper tool on the stem to which the gradient has already been applied and then apply it to the selected elements. Then move the objects to the back (Command/Ctrl + Shift + [).

ELEMENT 5
Adding Gradient Mesh Effects to the Petals

Step 1

Use the Group Selection tool to select the leaf. Set the Fill color in the Color palette as shown here. Choose Object, Create Gradient Mesh to open the Create Gradient Mesh dialog box and set the Rows to 8, the Columns to 3, and select To Center from the Appearance drop-down list. The center of the object will appear bright, while a mesh line appears inside the selected leaf.

Step 2

Use the Mesh tool to select a mesh point inside the stem and select the color in the Color palette as shown here. This will create a soft gradient around the selected mesh point. Select each of the other mesh points in turn and move the points or modify the direction line until the desired gradient is achieved.

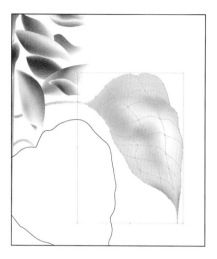

Step 3

Use the Group Selection tool to select the leaf, as shown here. Select the Fill color in the Color palette, as shown here. Choose Object, Create Gradient Mesh to open the Create Gradient Mesh dialog box and set the Rows to 8, the Columns to 5, and select Flat from the Appearance drop-down list. The center of the leaf will appear bright while a mesh line appears inside the selected leaf.

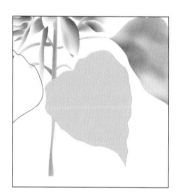
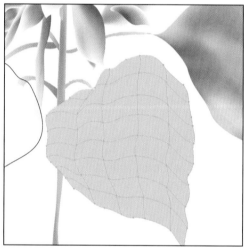

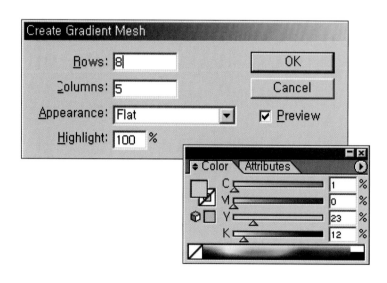

Step 4

Apply the gradient mesh to the other leaves.

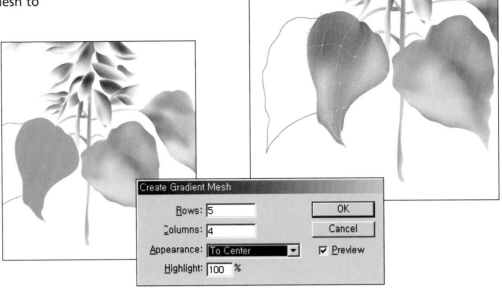

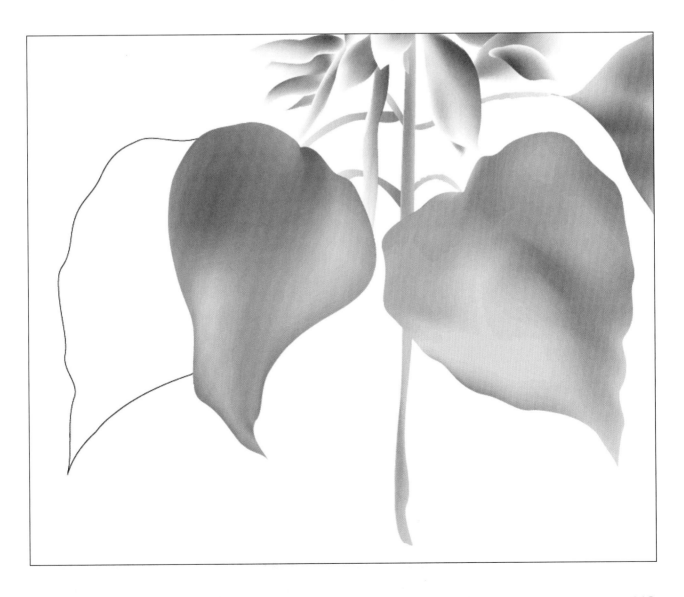

Step 5

This time, you will learn how to apply gradient mesh effects without using the Create Gradient Mesh dialog box. Selecting the Gradient Mesh tool and clicking on one area of the image will create web-like mesh lines where you clicked the mouse. Complete the image by altering the mesh lines and color until the desired result is achieved.

ELEMENT 6
Adding Natural Lines to Objects

Step 1

Use the Selection tool to select the duplicated line image and then press Command/Ctrl + C to copy it. Make a new layer in the Layers palette. Name the layer "flower line," and click OK.

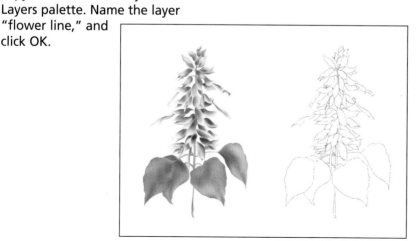
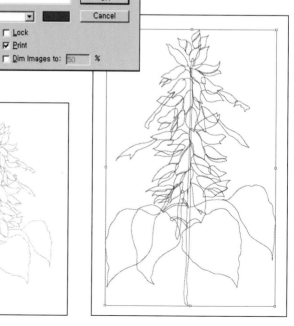

Step 2

Press Command/Ctrl + V to paste the copied image into the flower line layer and delete it from the flower layer. As shown here, select the copied line image and arrange it so that it fills up the entire page. Lock the flower layer in the Layers palette.

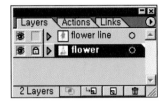

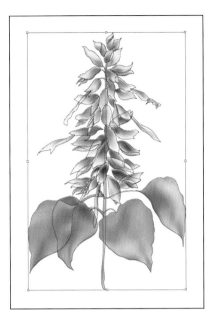 

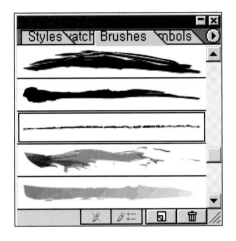

Step 3

Selecting the line image, select the Pencil brush from the Brushes palette and apply it to the line image. Select the Stroke color in the Color palette as shown here. In the Transparency palette, set the Opacity to 50% so that the borders appear faded.

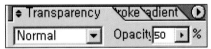

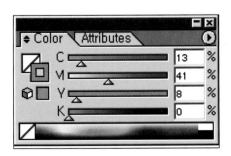

Step 4

Use the Selection tool to select several leaves, as shown here. Clicking the Eyedropper tool on leaves to which the brush has already been applied will apply it to the other selected leaves.

Step 5

Set the Blending Mode to Soft Light in the Transparency palette to make the object brighter than the original.

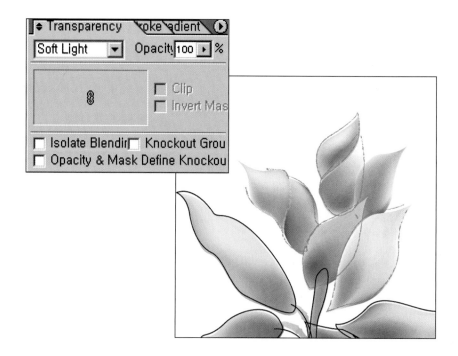

Step 6

Finish the rest of the leaves by selecting the leaves and clicking the Eyedropper tool on the leaves to which the brush has already been applied.

Step 7

Click and drag the Erase tool over the areas where the leaves overlap.

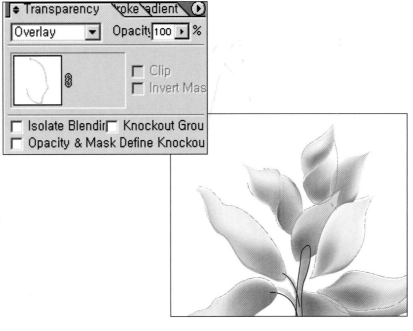

Step 8

In the Transparency palette, click the Option button and select Show Options. Select the flower and select Overlay from the Blending Mode pull-down list. Applying different Blending Modes changes the color of the image. Choose the Blending Mode value that creates the desired effect.

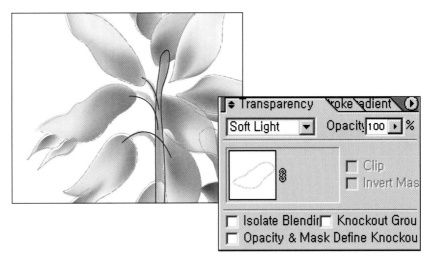

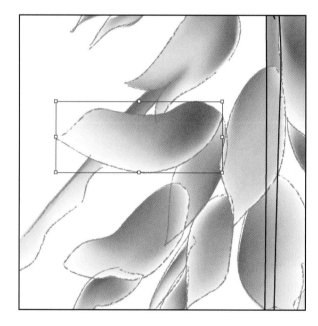

Step 9

Click the Eyedropper tool on the images to which the brush has already been applied. This applies the same effect to the other selected leaves. Click and drag the Erase tool over the areas where the leaves overlap.

ELEMENT 7
Drawing the Petal Veins

Step 1
Click the Eyedropper tool on the elements to which the brush has already been applied to apply it to the other selected objects. Select the Stroke Color in the Color palette as shown here.

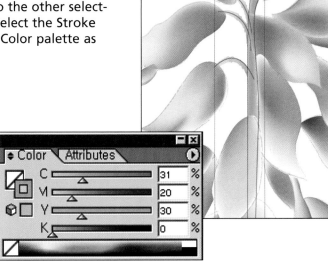

Step 2
Select the remaining elements of the stem and click the Eyedropper tool on the elements to which the brush has already been applied to apply the same brush effect.

Step 3

Click and drag the Erase tool over the areas where the objects overlap.

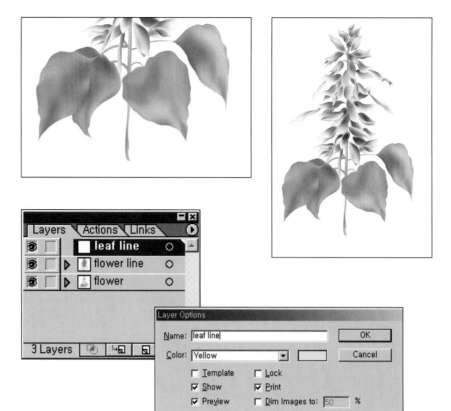

Step 4

Make a new layer in the Layers palette. Name the new layer "leaf line," and click OK.

Step 5

Set the Fill to None and the Stroke to black. Use the Pen tool to draw in the veins of the leaves as shown here.

Step 6

Select the leaf veins. Choose Window, Brush Libraries, Artistic Sample to open the Artistic Sample palette. In the Artistic Sample palette, select the Charcoal, Rough brush to apply the brush to the object.

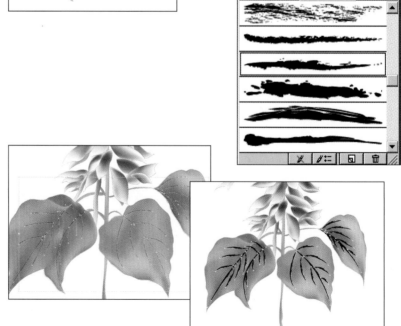

Step 7

Select the Stroke color in the Color palette to change the color of the black leaf veins to a lighter color.

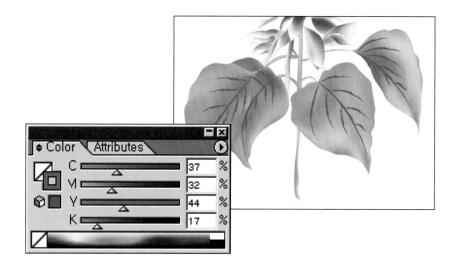

Step 8

In the Transparency palette, select Multiply from the Blending Mode pull-down list and set the Opacity to 25%.

Step 9

Click and drag the Erase tool over the areas where the objects overlap.

ELEMENT 8
Making Patterns and Applying Them to Objects

Step 1

Make a new layer from the Layers palette. Name the new layer "pattern," and click OK. Lock all the other layers so that only the pattern layer can be manipulated.

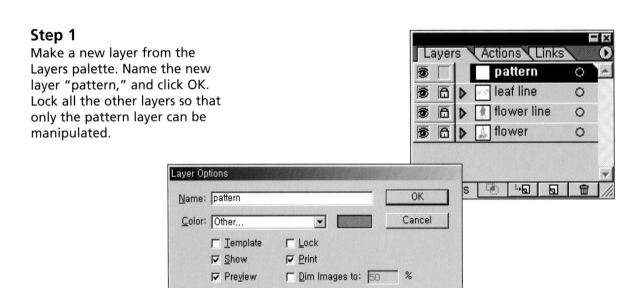

Step 2

Select the Polygon tool and then click an empty space in the image to open the Polygon dialog box. In the Polygon dialog box, set the Radius to 3pt and the Sides to 6, and click OK. Use the Zoom tool to zoom into the image and draw a hexagon.

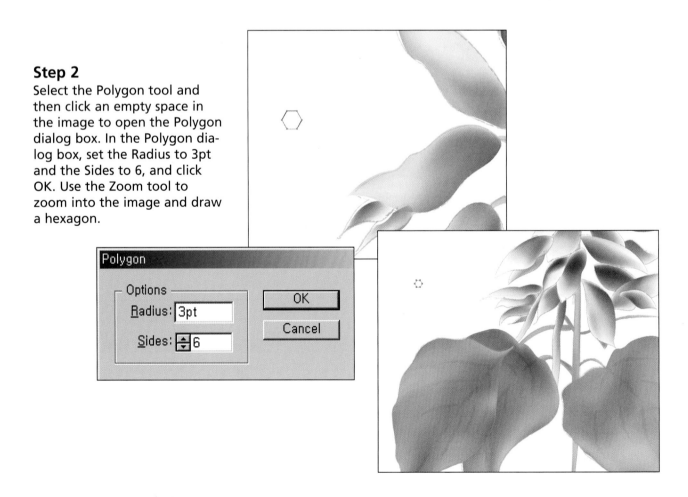

Step 3

Select the Stroke color in the Color palette, as shown here. In the Stroke dialog box, set the Weight to 0.1pt and the Cap to Round Cap. Then, choose Window, Swatches to open the Swatches palette. Using the Selection tool, drag the hexagon to the Swatches palette to register it as a pattern.

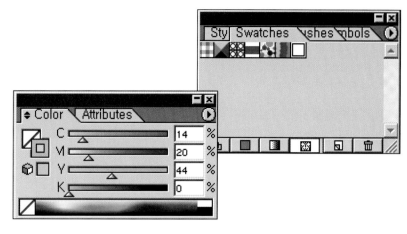

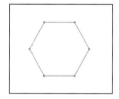

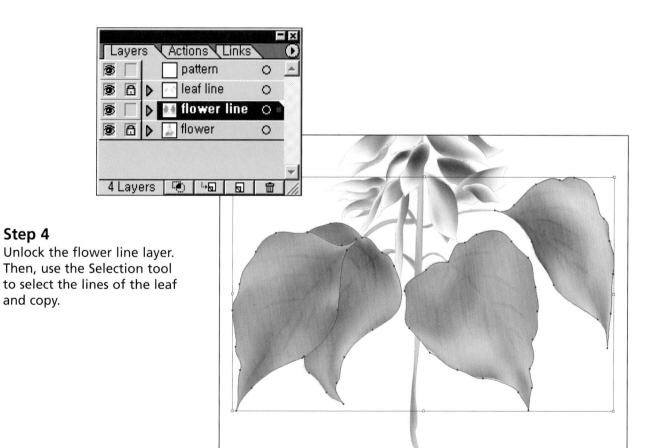

Step 4

Unlock the flower line layer. Then, use the Selection tool to select the lines of the leaf and copy.

Step 5

Select the pattern layer in the Layers palette, select Edit, Paste to paste the copied leaf lines (Command/Ctrl + V). Using the arrow keys on the keyboard, move the leaf lines to fit the leaves in the image.

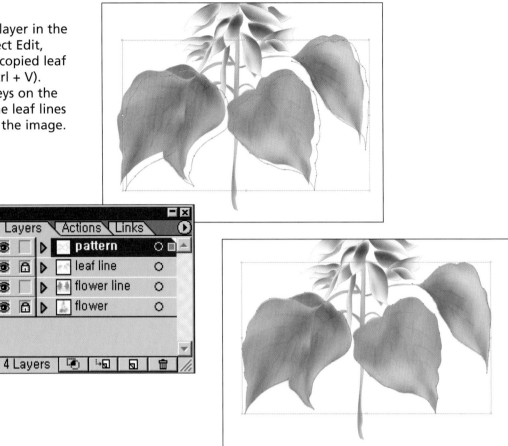

Step 6

Click and select the lines, and then select the hexagon pattern that was registered in the Swatches palette, apply it to the selected lines. This will apply a net-like pattern to the inside of the leaf as shown here.

Step 7

To adjust the size of the applied pattern, select the pattern object and right-click (Command-Click) the mouse to select Transform, Scale. In the Scale dialog box, check the Uniform checkbox and set the Scale to 80%. After checking only Patterns in Options, click OK to apply the configurations. We can see that the size of the pattern has gotten smaller.

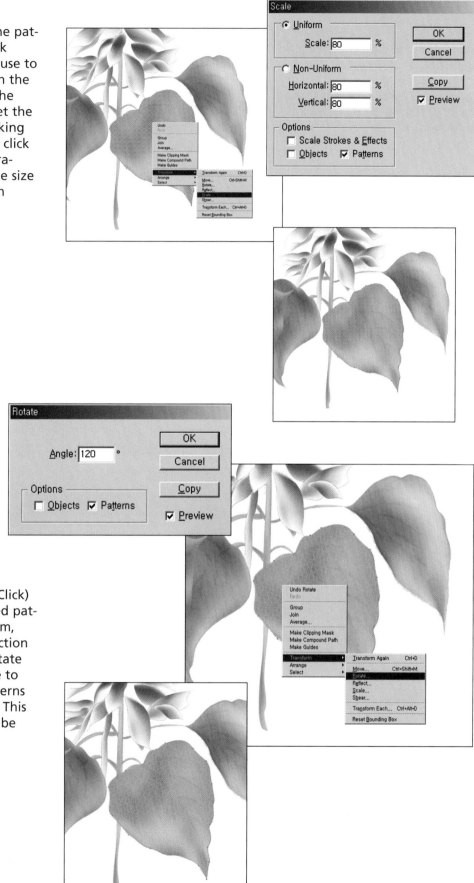

Step 8

Right-click (Command + Click) the mouse on the selected pattern and choose Transform, Rotate to adjust the direction of the pattern. In the Rotate dialog box, set the Angle to 120% and select the Patterns checkbox as shown here. This will cause the pattern to be placed on a diagonal.

Step 9

In the Transparency palette, set the Opacity to 67% to make the pattern transparent. Selecting another linear leaf, click the Eyedropper tool on a completed pattern to apply the same pattern directly to the selected leaf.

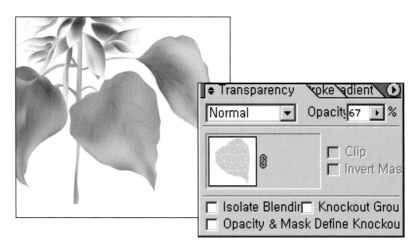

Project 4
Design of Editing

SALVIA SPLENDENS

Scarlet sage has an upright growth with spikes of bright flowers in shades of red. The flowers will bloom through summer and autumn if plants are cut back after each flowering flush. Most varieties grow to 10-12inches high, but there are cultivars that will grow to 20 inches. Salvia is best used in massed displays and as pot plants. It will not last long as a cut flower. Salvia prefers warm, tropical climates, but it can be grown in cooler areas if given protection from bad weather. It is not suitable for cold climates. Choose a hot, sunny location with well-drained soil. Enrich very poor or sandy soils with manure or compost ahead of planting. Some newer varieties will show bolder color if given light shade. Sow seeds in early spring in warm zones and in late spring in cooler areas. If starting indoors, transplant when seedlings are one to two inches high. Once the plants are established, water deeply every week or so. Plants will not tolerate soil that is constantly wet, and overwatering will cause the plant to collapse. Sidedress monthly to promote strong growth and good flowering. In tropical climates the plants can be cut back after flowering for a second season of blooms. carlet sage has an upright growth with spikes of bright flowers in shades of red. The flowers will bloom through summer and autumn if plants are cut back after each flowering flush. Most varieties grow to 10-12 inches high, but there are cultivars that will grow to 20 inches. Salvia is best used in massed displays and as pot plants. It will not last long as a cut flower. Salvia prefers warm, tropical climates, but it can be grown in cooler areas if given protection from bad weather. It is not suitable for cold climates. Choose a hot, sunny location with well-drained soil. Enrich very poor or sandy soils with manure or compost ahead of planting. Some newer varieties will show bolder color if given light shade. Sow seeds in early spring in warm zones and in late spring in cooler areas. If starting indoors, transplant when seedlings are one to two inches high. Once the plants are established, water deeply every week or so. Plants will not tolerate soil that is constantly wet, and overwatering will cause the plant to collapse. Sidedress monthly to promote strong growth and good flowering. In tropical climates the plants can be cut back after flowering for a second season of blooms.

Flower Guide

Type: annual
Propagation: seeds
Flower Color: shades of red
Bloom Time: all summer
Uses: massed displays, pots

PROJECT 4
Design of Editing

The type features of Illustrator are similar to those in word processors and QuarkXPress, but what makes Illustrator unique is its ability to integrate text and images. One of the advantages of Illustrator is the ability to convert entire text blocks to vector outlines for elaborate and detailed reshaping. You will use type features of Illustrator combined with design objects to create a complex illustration.

Source Files

Frame.ai

Salvia(G).ai

ELEMENT 1
Making Frame Objects and Dotted Lines

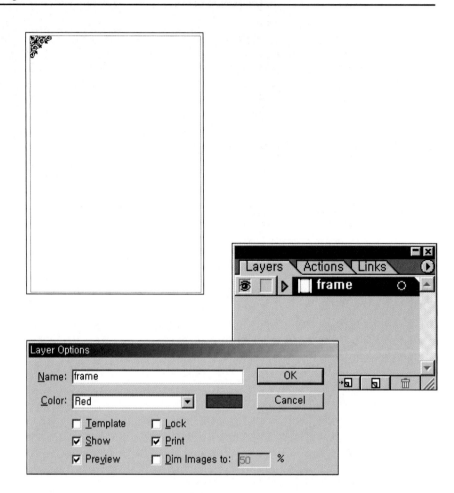

Step 1
Choose File, Open from the menu bar to open the FRAME.AI image. In the Open dialog box, follow this file folder path on the supplementary CD-ROM: BOOK_10/PROJECT04/SOURCE/FRAME.AI. Open the FRAME.AI image (Command/Ctrl + O).

Step 2
Rename layer 1 "frame," as shown here.

Step 3
Select the frame element using the Selection tool from the toolbox and choose View, Show Rulers (Command/Ctrl + R). To define the middle of the page, choose View, Guides, Show Guides (Command/Ctrl + ;). Click and drag the ruler on the left to the middle to create a vertical guide in the center of the page.

Step 4

Use the Reflect tool to move the center point to the middle. Holding down the Shift and Option/Alt keys, drag the selected frame element to the right to make a copy.

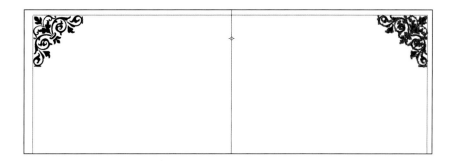

Step 5

Use the Line Segment tool to draw in a line between the two frames, as shown here.

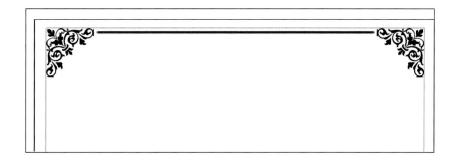

Step 6

Choose Window, Stroke to open the Stroke palette (F10). In the Stroke palette, click the Option button and select Show Options to reveal a menu that will allow you to adjust the line in more detail. Set the Weight to 3pt and the Cap to Butt Cap. Select the Dashed Line checkbox, type 3pt in the dash box and 4pt in the gap box. The line is now a dashed line. This kind of dashed-line configuration will allow us to create a variety of different linear shapes.

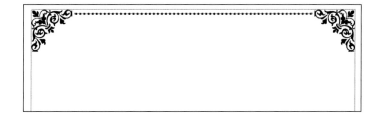

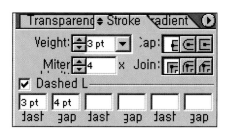

ELEMENT 2
Completing the Frame Object

Step 1

Click and drag the ruler at the top to the center to create a horizontal guide in the center of the page. To lock the guides, select View, Guides, Lock Guides (Command/Ctrl + Option/Alt + ;).

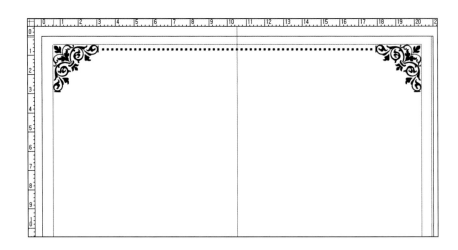

Step 2

Using the Selection tool, click and drag over the top frame element to select it. Use the Reflect tool to bring the center point to the center of the page. Holding down the Shift and Option/Alt keys, drag the selected frame element to make a copy.

Step 3

Use the Line Segment tool to draw in a vertical line between the two frames, as shown here. Set the Weight to 3pt and the Cap to Butt Cap. Select the Dashed Line checkbox, type 3pt in the dash box and 4pt in the gap box. The line is now a dashed line.

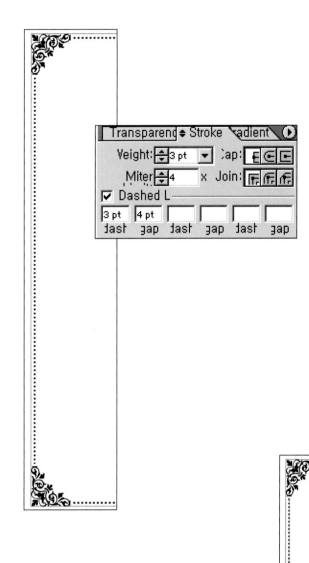

Step 4

With the vertical dashed line selected, use the Reflect tool to move center point of the line to the middle of the page. Holding down the Shift and Option/Alt keys, drag the selected line to make a copy. Hide the guides (Command/Ctrl + ;).

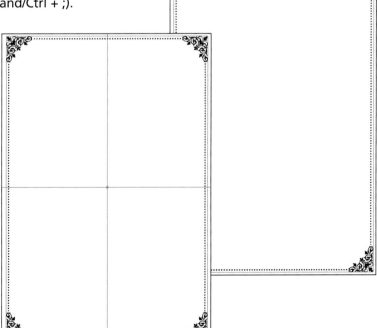

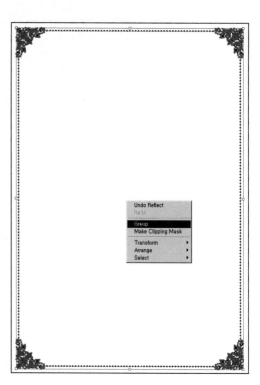

Step 5

Choose View, Hide Page Tiling
to hide the tiling lines. Use the
Selection tool to select the
entire frame and then right-
click (Command + Click) the
mouse and select Group to
group the selected elements.

ELEMENT 3
Arranging the Flower Image &
Configuring the Frame Color

Step 1
Choose File, Open to open the SALVIA(G).ai image. In the Open dialog box, follow this file folder path from the supplementary CD-ROM: BOOK_10/PROJECT04/SOURCE/SALVIA(G).AI. Open the SALVIA(G).AI image (Command/Ctrl + O).

Step 2
Copy the SALVIA(G).AI image (Command/Ctrl + C). Paste the copied SALVIA(G).AI image into the FRAME.AI document.

Step 3
Create a new layer in the Layers palette and name the new layer "flower."

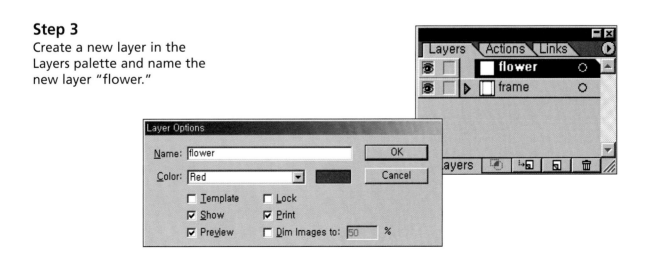

Step 4

Lock the flower layer. Select the frame image and choose Object, Ungroup to undo the grouping of the elements (Command/Ctrl + Shift + G).

Step 5

Select the four frame elements situated in each of the corners. To select several elements at the same time, select one element while holding down the Shift key and then clicking on the remaining three elements. To adjust the color, choose Window, Color to open the Color palette (F6). Set the Fill color, as shown here. Select the four dashed lines and set the Stroke color, as shown here.

Step 6

Use the Selection tool to select the flower image and move it to the lower right-hand side of the screen, as shown here.

ELEMENT 4
Making a Classic Name Bar

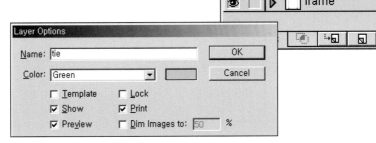

Step 1

Make a new layer and name it "tie."

Step 2

Draw the image shown here using the Pen tool. First, sketch the image on paper, scan it into the computer, and paste it into a template layer. Templates use neighboring computer equipment to easily create a more polished image. (The completed Name Bar image is supplied in the supplementary CD-ROM.)

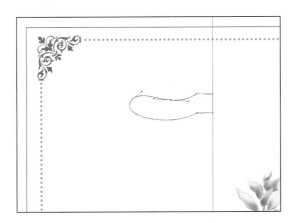

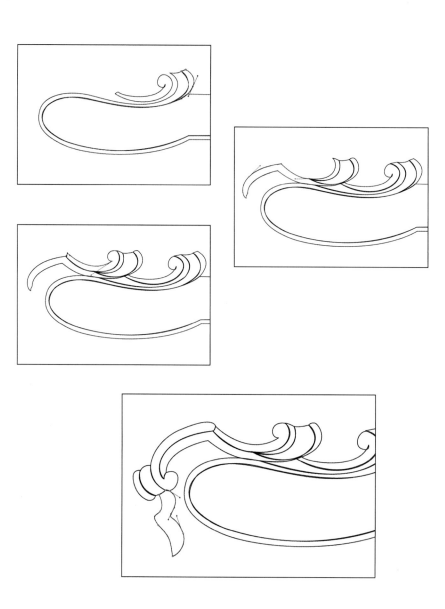

Step 3

When using the Pen tool, holding down the Command/Ctrl key while clicking and dragging allows you to select the anchor point and move it in the desired direction without having to use the Direct Selection tool. Use the Convert Anchor Point tool while holding down the Option/Alt key. Holding down the Command/Ctrl key and pressing the Tab key will select the Selection tool. Similarly, when using the Selection tool, holding down the Command/Ctrl key and pressing the Tab key will select the Direct Selection tool. The Selection tool is the most frequently used tool in Illustrator, and using shortcut keys makes for more efficient work.

Step 4

Use the Pen tool to draw the closed curve shapes one at a time to complete the Name Bar image.

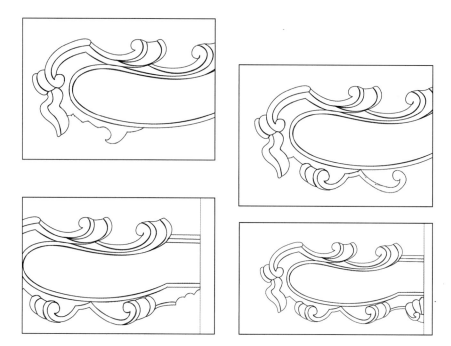

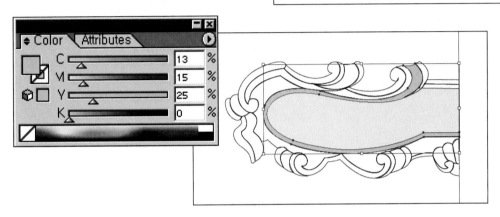

Step 5

Select one of the elements and set the Fill color, as shown here.

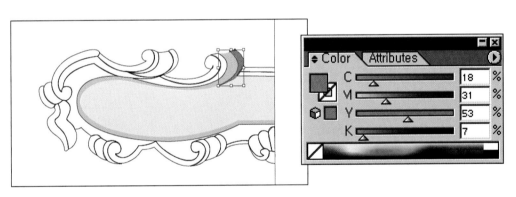

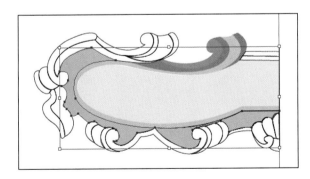

Step 6

Repeat Step 5, and set the Fill color for each of the elements, as shown here.

ELEMENT 5
Completing the Classic Name Bar

Step 1

Use the Blend tool to make solid elements. First, use the Selection tool to select two elements to which you will apply the Blend tool. Select the Blend tool and select one anchor point from one element and another anchor point on another. The Blend effect will be applied between the two selected anchor points.

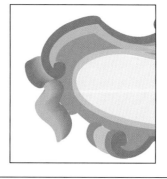

Step 2

Repeat Step 1 to apply the Blend tool to different portions of the image.

Step 3

Select the areas to which the Blend tool has not been applied, and set the Stroke color, as shown here.

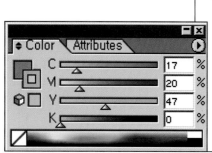

Step 4

Choose Window, Swatches to open the Swatches palette. Drag the Stroke color assigned in the Color palette to the Swatches palette to register the color. By registering the color in the Swatches palette, you can apply the same color to several different elements.

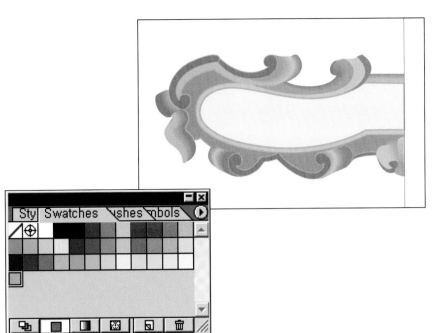

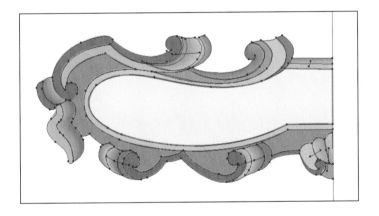

Step 5

Drag the Selection tool over the entire element to select it. Use the Reflect tool to place the center point as shown here. Drag while holding down the Shift and Option/Alt keys to make a symmetrical copy, as shown here.

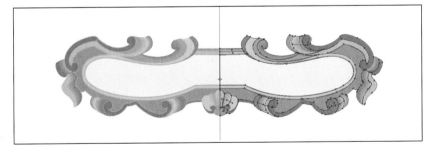

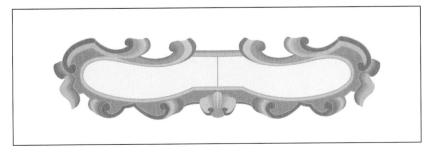

Step 6

Use the Selection tool to select the two elements, as shown here. Select Window, Pathfinder to open the Pathfinder palette and select the Add to shape area button to combine the two elements.

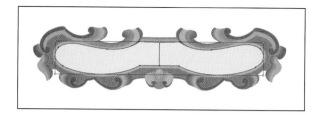

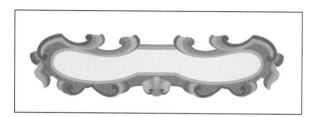

Step 7

Select the entire Name Bar image. Right-click (Command + Click) the mouse and select Group. The completed Name Bar image is shown here.

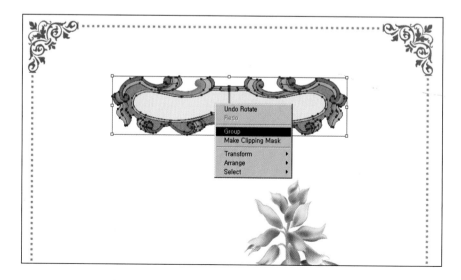

ELEMENT 6
Entering Text & Adding Shadow Effects

Step 1
Make a new layer and name it "text."

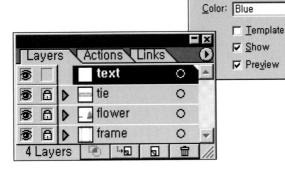

Step 2
Select the Type tool and type "Salvia Splendens."

Step 3
Choose Window, Type, Character to open the Character palette (Command/Ctrl + T). In the Character palette, specify the Font and Size, as shown here.

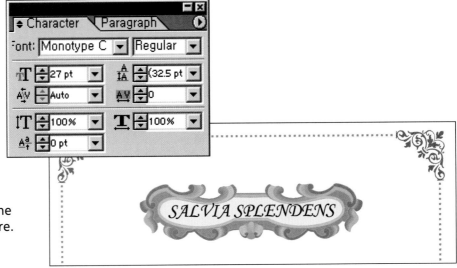

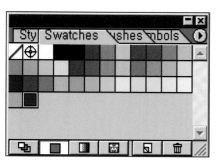

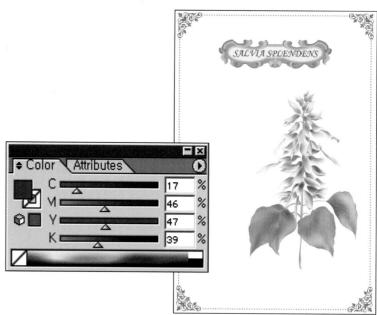

Step 4

With the text selected, set the Fill color, as shown here.

Step 5

Select the Name Bar image. Choose Effect, Stylize, Drop Shadow and assign each of the values shown here in the Drop Shadow dialog box.

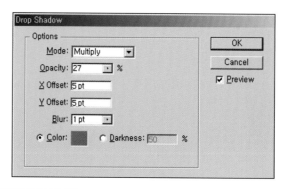

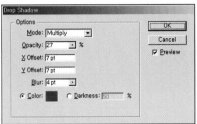

Step 6

Select the flower image. Choose Effect, Stylize, Drop Shadow and assign each of the values shown here in the Drop Shadow dialog box.

Step 7

The Drop Shadow effect gives a 3-dimensional effect to the Name Bar and flower images.

ELEMENT 7
Arranging Unique Text

Step 1

Choose File, Open and load the BOOK_10/PROJECT04/ SOURCE/TEXT.AI file from the supplementary CD-ROM (Command/Ctrl + O).

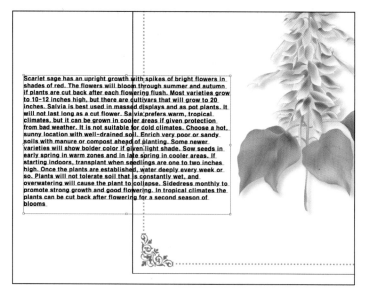

Step 2

Copy the text onto the clipboard. Draw a rectangular marquee with the Type tool, and paste the text into the type box.

Step 3

Use the Rectangle tool to draw a rectangle on the left-hand side of the screen, as shown here. Then, use the Ellipse tool to draw a vertical ellipse that extends from one corner of the rectangle to the other.

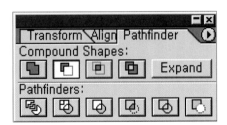

Step 4

Use the Selection tool to select the rectangle and the ellipse. Select Window, Pathfinder to open the Pathfinder palette (Shift + F9) and select the Subtract from shape area button to create the result shown here.

Step 5

Click the Expand button in the Pathfinder palette to make it into a separate element.

Step 6

Select the text and copy it. Then, select the Area Type tool from the toolbox, click the top left corner of the shape that you just made. This will remove the black fill color to leave behind only an outline of the original shape; an I-beam text cursor will appear where the mouse was clicked, allowing you to enter text.

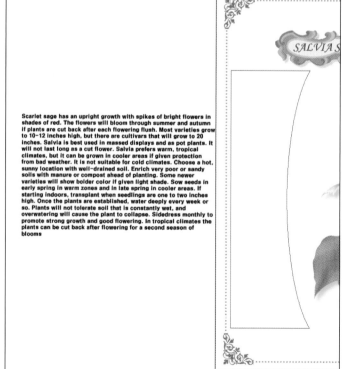

Step 7

Press Command/Ctrl + V to paste the copied text into the shape.

Step 8

Selecting the first letter S, adjust the font size in the Character palette, as shown here.

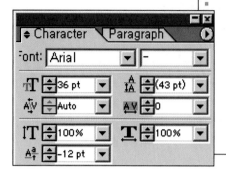

Step 9

Set the Baseline Shift to -12pt so that the letter S drops down. Use the Enter key and Space Bar to move the text in the second row so that it doesn't overlap with the letter S.

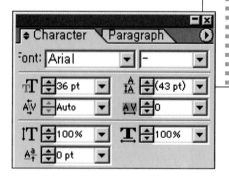

Step 10

Choose Window, Type, Paragraph to open the Paragraph palette (Command/Ctrl + M). Open the Options menu. Align the text by clicking the Justify All Lines button and select the Auto-Hyphenate and Hang Punctuation checkboxes.

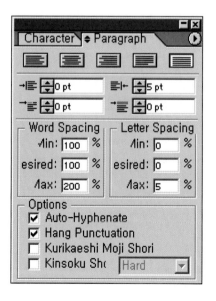

ELEMENT 8
Changing Text to Images and Configuring Color

Step 1
Change the color of the text to the Fill color shown here.

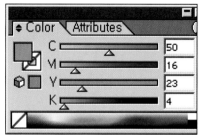

Step 2
Select the letter S, and set the Font to Times New Roman, Bold in the Character palette.

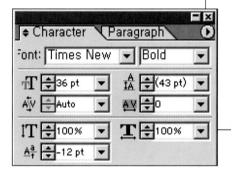

Step 3
Select the text and choose Type, Create Outlines (Command/Ctrl + Shift + O). This will convert the text to an image, allowing you to edit the text as you wish. Right-click (Command + Click) and select Ungroup to undo the grouping.

Step 4

Select the first line of text. Using the right arrow key (‡), move the selected element slightly to the right.

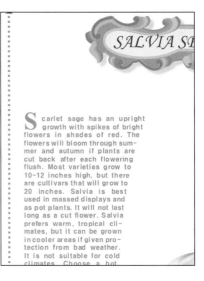

Step 5

Select the text, right-click (Command + Click) and select Group. Choose Window, Transparency to open the Transparency palette and set the Opacity to 60%.

ELEMENT 9
Making the Flower Guide

Step 1
Select the Type tool and type "Flower Guide" below the flower. Change the color of the text, as shown here.

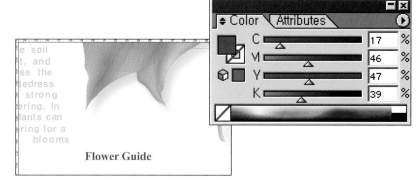

Step 2
Draw a rectangle next to the text and set the Fill color, as shown here.

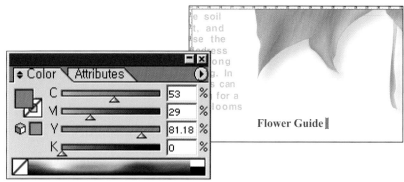

Step 3
Draw a line and set the Stroke color as shown here. Open the Options menu in the Stroke palette. Set the Weight to 0.75pt and the Cap to Butt Cap. After selecting the Dashed Line checkbox, set the dash box to 1pt.

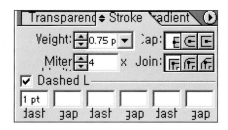

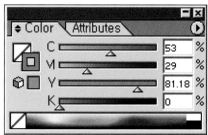

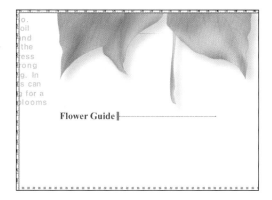

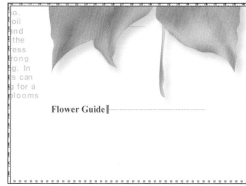

Step 4

Select the Type tool and enter the text "Type: annual, Propagation: seeds, Flower Color..." Set the Font and Size in the Character palette and adjust the Fill color, as shown here.

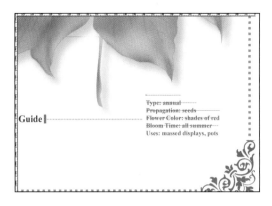

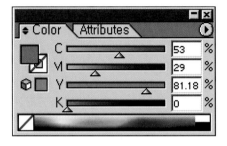

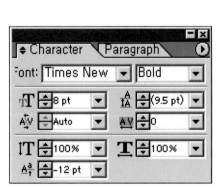

Step 5

Selecting the Rounded Rectangle tool and clicking on an empty space on the screen will create the Rounded Rectangle dialog box. In the Rounded Rectangle dialog box, enter the values for the Width, Height, and Corner Radius, as shown here.

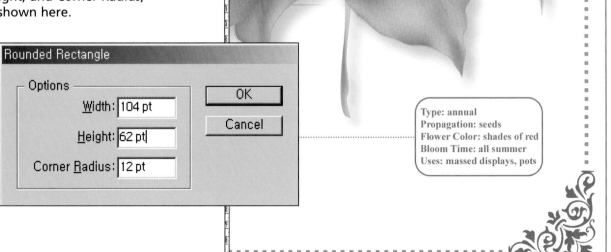

ELEMENT 10
Completing the Logo and Background

Step 1

In the Stroke palette, set the Weight to 1pt, and then set the Stroke color, as shown here.

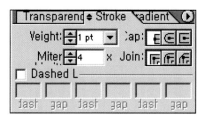

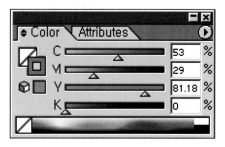

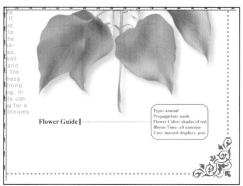

Step 2

Use the Type tool to enter "© FlowerGuides.2001 –Shannon@flower-guides.com" at the bottom of the image. Apply the color that has been registered previously in the Swatches palette.

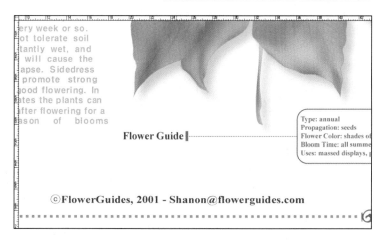

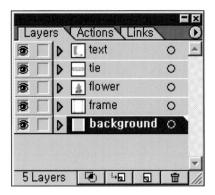

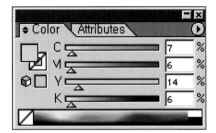

Step 3

Make a new layer and name it "background." Move this background layer to the very bottom of the Layers palette. Set the Fill color and use the Rectangle tool to draw a rectangle to fit the screen, as shown here. The background color gives the image a unique look.

SALVIA SPLENDENS

Scarlet sage has an upright growth with spikes of bright flowers in shades of red. The flowers will bloo through summer and autumn if plants are cut back after each flowering flush. Most varieties grow to 10-12inches high, but there are cultivars that will grow to 20 inches. Salvia is best used in massed displays and as pot plants. It will not last long as a cut flower. Salvia prefers warm, tropical climates, but it can be grown in cooler areas if given protection from bad weather. It is not suitable for cold climates. Choose a hot, sunny location with well-drained soil. Enrich very poor or sandy soils with manure or compost ahead of planting. Some newer varieties will show bolder color if given light shade. Sow seeds in early spring in warm zones and in late spring in cooler areas. If starting indoors, transplant when seedlings are one to two inches high. Once the plants are established, water deeply every week or so. Plants will not tolerate soil that is constantly wet, and overwatering will cause the plant to collapse. Sidedress monthly to promote strong growth and good flowering. In tropical climates the plants can be cut back after flowering for a second season of blooms. carlet sage has an upright growth with spikes of bright flowers in shades of red. The flowers will bloom through summer and autumn if plants are cut back after each flowering flush. Most varieties grow to 10-12 inches high, but there are cultivars that will grow to 20 inches. Salvia is best used in massed displays and as pot plants. It will not last long as a cut flower. Salvia prefers warm, tropical climates, but it can be grown in cooler areas if given protection from bad weather. It is not suitable for cold climates. Choose a hot, sunny location with well-drained soil. Enrich very poor or sandy soils with manure or compost ahead of planting. Some newer varieties will show bolder color if given light shade. Sow seeds in early spring in warm zones and in late spring in cooler areas. If starting indoors, transplant when seedlings are one to two inches high. Once the plants are established, water deeply every week or so. Plants will not tolerate soil that is constantly wet, and overwatering will cause the plant to collapse. Sidedress monthly to promote strong growth and good flowering. In tropical climates the plants can be cut back after flowering for a second season of blooms.

Flower Guide

Type: annual
Propagation: seeds
Flower Color: shades of red
Bloom Time: all summer
Uses: massed displays, pots

Project 5
Tourism Brochure Design

Tourism

Ancient Egypt

Exhibitions
Activities & Events
Tourist Information
Resources for Researcher
visitor information

EGYPT

The tourist balance between Egypt and Britain swings down strongly on the side of Egypt, with numbers of visiting British much greater than that of Egyptians visiting the United Kingdom. In so far as interests are concerned, the balance is way off the scale.

But the future for a two-way traffic flow looks bright. Industry members are assessing the requirements of each, and asking why the British come to Egypt, and what is the main attraction of the UK for Egyptians?

Britain is currently fourth on the list of countries sending tourists to Egypt, with 180,904 visitors to the land of the Pharaohs in the first half of this year. This, Egyptian tourist officials say, is an increase of 5.5 per cent over the same period last year.

If one looks at the number of Egyptians travelling to the UK, as British Embassy officials comment, "statistics don't talk."

"I would say that 70 to 80 per cent of the 30,000 visa applications to the UK annually are for tourism. I have no definite number," British Embassy Consul in Cairo Gordon Brown told Al-Ahram Weekly.

There are historical reasons for the discrepancy in numbers. While tourism from the UK to Egypt began well over a century ago, tourists only began trickling from Egypt to the UK in the late 1970s. Egyptians who tour abroad make up a relatively small number of the population, the main cause of this being the financial factor. Furthermore, the currency exchange rates are an obstacle for many. Let us not forget, either, that obtaining a visa is no easy matter.

This is not the only reason for the one-way flow of tourists. British tourists often visit Egypt in groups arranged by travel agencies, and this is a long-established business. Major travel agencies organising holidays to Egypt are Thomas Cook, Thompson, Kuoni, Bales and Zomack, all offering packages at competitive prices. Egyptians, on the other hand, tend to travel to the UK as individuals, and consequently do not benefit from package prices. True, Egyptian travel agents have become aware in recent years that, among the increasing numbers of Egyptians who want to holiday in UK, are many who might be interested

in the financial advantages of organised trips, but this has not yet become a trend.

Another interesting difference is goals. British tourists are called the "Lovers of Luxor." "Lovers of the Nile" and "Fans of Egyptian Monuments and Culture." Egyptians want to shop. Hardly any Egypt-ian can be found at the Tower of London, but you will find them in large numbers in Oxford Street. The British come to Egypt on package tours to see the sites, but don't spend much on other things. Egyptians go to England to spend, spend, spend!

Britain's love affair with Egypt, if one can call it that, goes back to 1869 when Thomas Cook recognis-ed that the best way to see the country's historical sites was by boat and introduced the first paddle-steamer tour. The publication of Amelia Edwards A

PROJECT 5
Tourism Brochure Design

One of the most outstanding features of Illustrator

is its ability to complete precise and detailed images.

Basic figures are used to design patterns and then these

patterns are applied to images. You will use Illustrator's

Effect features to design a tourism brochure.

Source Files

Wallpainting.jpg

Pyramid.jpg

EG_map.jpg

Wallpainting.ai

map.ai

ELEMENT 1
Converting the Egyptian Mural into a Template

Step 1

Open a new document (Command/Ctrl + N). In the New Document dialog box, type "wallpainting" in the Name area, 210mm in the Width area, and 297mm in the Height area. Select the CMYK Color radio button, and then click OK.

Step 2

Load the Egyptian Mural image by choosing File, Place. In the Place dialog box, select the BOOK_10/PROJECT05/SOURCE/WALL-PAINTING.JPG file from the supplementary CD-ROM and load the image.

Step 3

To use the wallpainting image as a template, double-click the Layer 1 layer to open the Layer Options dialog box. Type "men" in the Name area and select the Template checkbox. By selecting the Template checkbox the men layer converts to a template layer to be used as the background image.

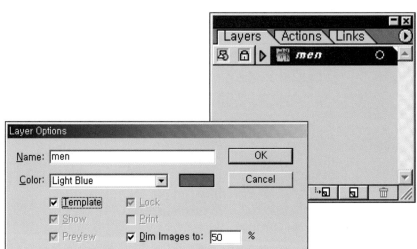

Step 4

The WALLPAINTING.JPG image has been established as the template screen. Converting the loaded image into a template will prevent the image from being affected by the use of any tool while working in Illustrator and will allow you to use it as a fixed background image.

ELEMENT 2
Adding Gradient Mesh Effects to the Petals

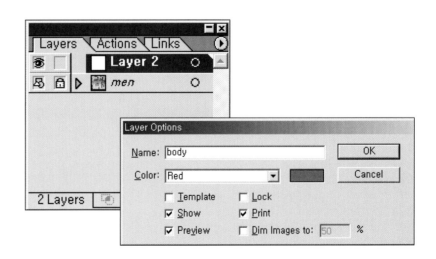

Step 1

Create a new layer in the Layers palette and name it "body."

Step 2

Set the Fill and Stroke colors, as shown here.

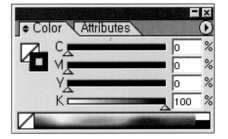

Step 3

Outline the background image using the Pen tool. First verify which areas will use the same color and then outline, in order, the body, the face and the hands. When outlining the curves, adjust the direction of the lines as shown here. Leaving the lateral direction lines alone, click and drag on the next anchor point to draw a smooth curve. To modify the curve of a line, click Command/Ctrl to temporarily convert the Selection tool to the Direct Selection tool to modify the direction lines while making the modifications. To deselect the image, hold down the Command/Ctrl key while pressing on an empty space on the screen.

Step 4

To outline the shape of the legs, first zoom into this area. To zoom into a certain area of an image, use the Zoom tool or use the Command/Ctrl key and Space Bar. To zoom back out, press Command/Ctrl + Space Bar + Option/Alt.

Step 5

To draw the curves, click and drag on the next anchor point and adjust the direction line that appears to fit it to the shape. Bring the Pen tool back to the starting point to create a closed image. To modify the line, press the Command/Ctrl key to convert to the Direct Selection tool to select the area that will be modified. When the direction line appears where the lines connect, hold down the Command/Ctrl key to adjust the direction line to fit the shape. If unnecessary anchor points appear on the line, remove them using the Delete Anchor Point tool or add them using the Add Anchor Point tool.

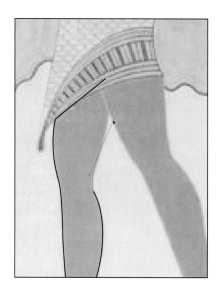
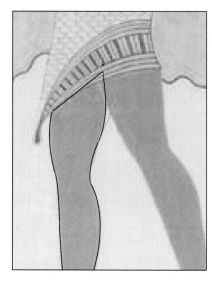

Step 6

Finish outlining the image, as shown here. To see if the lines have been drawn correctly, select View, Outline to preview the outline path. You have now completed the overall shape of the body (body, arms, and legs).

Step 7

Use the Pen tool to draw in the details as closed paths, such as the toenails and the anklet.

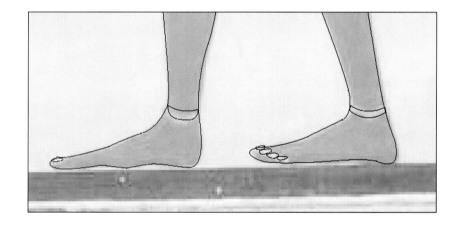

Step 8

The eyes in the mural are all the same size and shape, so copy and paste them. First, hold down the Command/Ctrl key to select the outlined eye. While holding down the Command/Ctrl key, drag the selected eye to the desired location and then press the Option/Alt key to copy it.

Step 9

To make the head, make a new layer and name it "hair."

Step 10

Repeat Steps 3, 4, and 5 to outline the shape of the hair. Select the hair, set the Fill color to black and the Stroke color to None. These settings will make the hair black, as shown here.

Step 11

Repeat Step 10 to draw the hair on the second man. Select the hair and then click the Eyedropper tool on the hair of the first man to apply the same color to the second man. The hair color of both men is now the same.

Step 12

To draw the vase that both men are holding, make a new layer and name it "bottle."

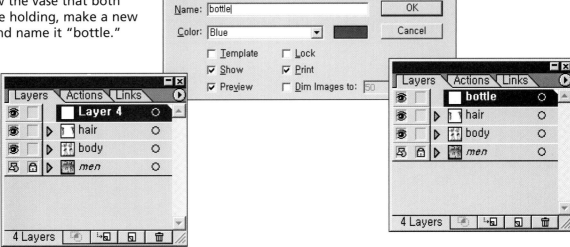

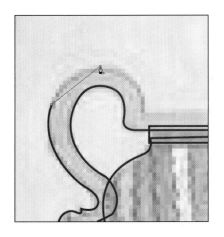
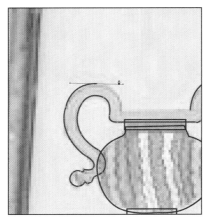

Step 13

Repeat Steps 3-5 to outline the vase.

Step 14

Draw in the hemline of the skirts, as shown here. You have now completed the outline. To see if the lines have been drawn correctly, select View, Outline to preview the overall image (Command/Ctrl + Y).

ELEMENT 3
Using the Color Palette to Add Color

Step 1
Select the Selection tool. When working with another tool, press the Command/Ctrl key to convert to the Selection tool. To apply the Selection tool to several images at a time, after selecting the first image, hold down the Shift key and then make the other selections.

Step 2
Select the Fill color in the tool-box. Make a brick-like color by adjusting each of the CMYK values in the Color palette. Set the Stroke to black. The same color will be applied to all selected elements.

Step 3
Select all the elements to which the same color will be applied by first selecting the first element and then holding down the Shift key to make the other selections.

Step 4
Use the Eyedropper tool to select the brick color of the first man and apply it to the second man, as shown here.

Step 5

Select the vases and apply color to them, as shown here.

Step 6

Use the Pen tool to draw in lines on the vase held by the first man. Selecting each of the lines, apply a color, as shown here.

Step 7

To fill in the hemline of the skirt with a gradient color, select the Gradient tool. Open the Gradient palette by choosing Window, Gradient (F9). When a color is selected, a triangular color tab will appear below the gradient spectrum. After selecting each of the spectrum tabs, adjust the CMYK values in the Color palette to create the desired color. Select Linear from the Type pull-down list, and then drag the gradient to the Swatches palette to save.

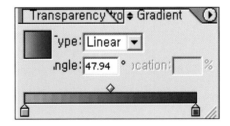

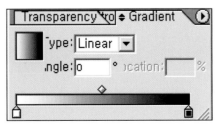
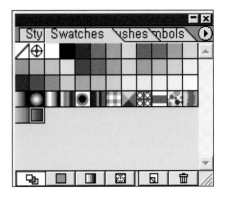

Step 8

Select the element to which you will apply the gradient color. Then, apply the gradient just saved in the Swatches palette to the selected elements. Adjust the direction of the gradient until the desired result is attained. The degree of spread and angle of the color depends on the direction and length of the click and drag. A long click and drag will create a wide and natural color.

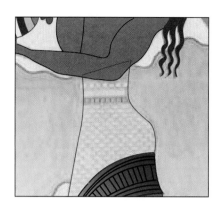

Step 9

Repeat Step 7 to make the other gradient color, as shown here, and then save it in the Swatches palette. Using the registered gradient color, fill in the hemline of the skirt.

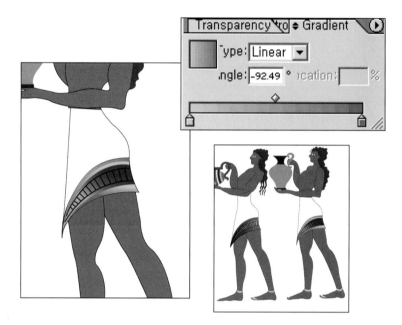

ELEMENT 4
Making a Pattern to Fill in the Color of the Skirts

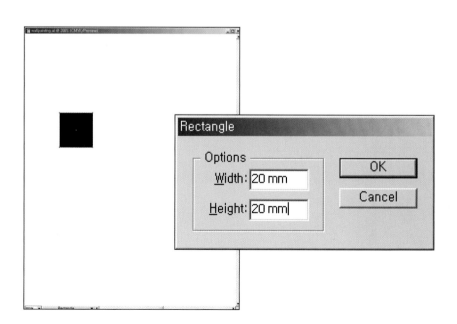

Step 1

In order to fill in the color of the skirt using a pattern, you first need to make the pattern. Select the Rectangle tool and click an empty space on the screen to open the Rectangle dialog box. In this dialog box, set both the Width and Height to 20mm to make a square.

Step 2

To make the dimensions for the pattern, create a square grid. Right-click (Command + Click) on the 20mm X 20mm square while holding down the Command/Ctrl key and select Transform, Move to open the Move dialog box (Command/Ctrl + Shift + N). Type 20mm in the Horizontal area and 0mm in the Vertical area, and then click OK.

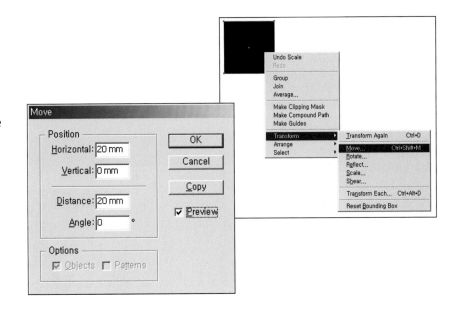

Step 3

The previous step will create two adjacent, square images. Right-click (Command + Click) and select Transform, Transform Again to repeat the Move command (Command/Ctrl + D).

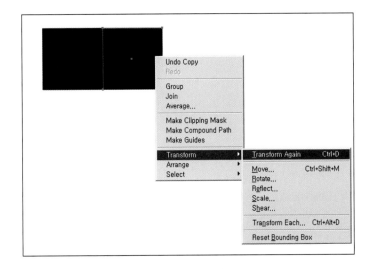

Step 4

Select all four square images that have been made. Right-click (Command + Click) and select Transform, Move to open the Move dialog box. Type 0mm in the Horizontal area and 20mm in the Vertical area, and then click OK.

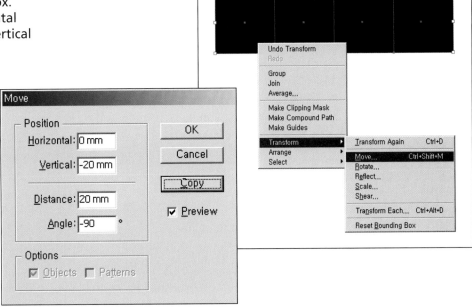

Step 5

This creates eight square images. Click and drag the Selection tool to select all eight square images. Choose View, Guides, Make Guides to make the guide that will serve as the foundation for the skirt pattern.

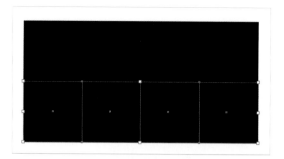

Step 6

When drawing the pattern source, select View, Smart Guides so that the pattern is drawn precisely within the guides (Command/Ctrl + U).

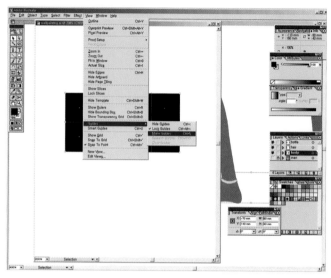

Step 7

Select the Rectangle tool and draw a rectangle (Width 40mm X Height 20mm) that fits precisely in the guide. Right-click (Command + Click) and select Transform, Move. In the Move dialog box, type 10mm in the Horizontal area and 20mm in the Vertical area, and then click OK.

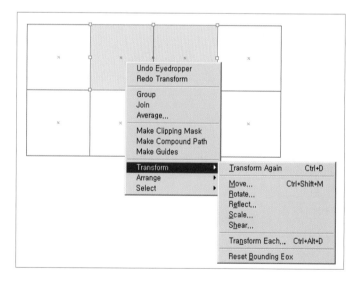

Step 8

Using the Pen tool, draw the closed triangles inside the square, as shown here.

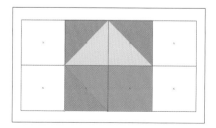

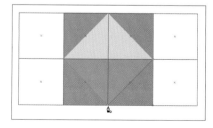

Step 9

To make a repeating pattern, make the two triangles on the top and bottom the same color. Select both triangles on the top. In the Color palette, adjust Fill color, as shown here. Select the two triangles on the bottom and apply a color. You have now completed the image that will be used as the repeating pattern.

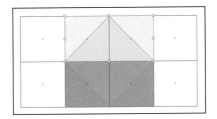

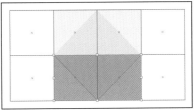

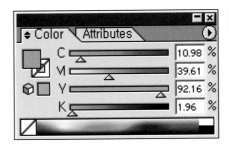

Step 10

Use the Selection tool to select the entire pattern. Drag this pattern onto the Swatch palette to save it.

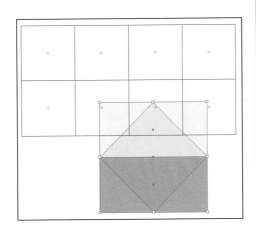

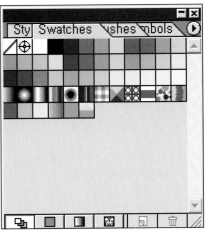

Step 11

Select the skirt of the man while holding down the Command/Ctrl key. Make the Fill active and select the pattern saved in the Swatches palette to apply it to the skirt.

Step 12

To reduce the size of the pattern, right-click (Command + Click) and select Transform, Scale. Choose Preview to view the changes made to the image. In the Scale dialog box, set the Scale to 5%, deselect Images, and select Pattern. The size of the pattern will get smaller while the size of the image will remain the same. Adjust the size of the pattern while previewing the image to make the most appropriate size.

Step 13

Right-click (Command + Click) on the skirt image and select Arrange, Send to Back so that the skirt is positioned in the back (Command/Ctrl + Shift + [).

Step 14

Change the color of the pattern source to make a new pattern, as shown here. Then save this new pattern in the Swatches palette.

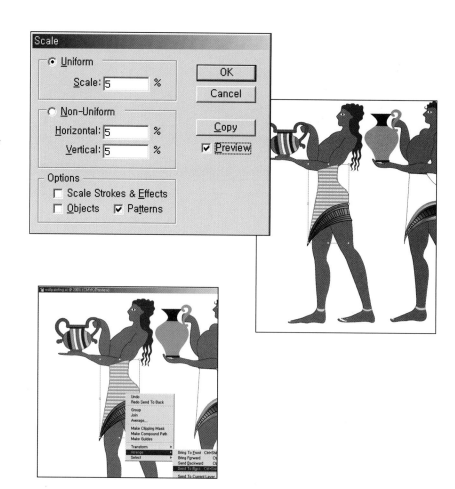

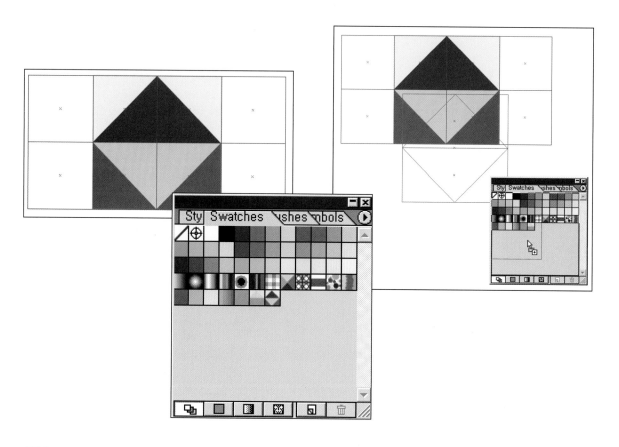

Step 15

Select the skirt on the right while holding down the Command/Ctrl key. Make Fill active and select the new pattern in the Swatches palette.

Step 16

To reduce the size of the pattern, right-click (Command + Click) and select Transform, Scale. Choose Preview to view the changes made to the image. In the Scale dialog box, set the Scale to 5%, deselect Images, and select Pattern. Only the size of the pattern will become smaller while the size of the image will remain the same. Adjust the size of the pattern while previewing the image to make the most appropriate size.

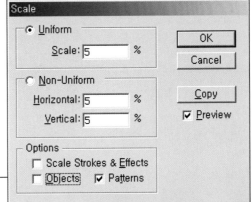

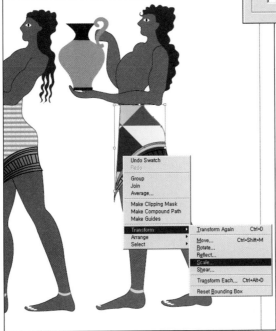

Step 17

Finally, adjust the color to complete the mural, as shown here. Select the images to which the color will be modified while holding down the Command/Ctrl key and then press the Shift key to select several images at the same time. Set the Stroke and Fill colors, as shown here.

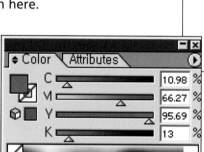

Step 18

You have now completed the mural image. Drag the men layer to the trash. Press Command/Ctrl + S to save the image.

ELEMENT 5
Making the Tourism Brochures Design Work Screen

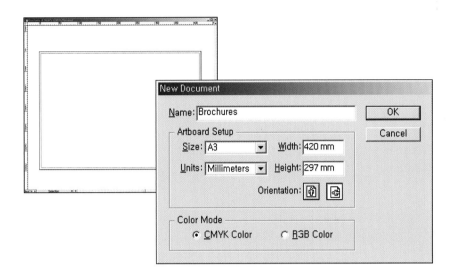

Step 1

Make a new document and name it "Brochures." Enter 420mm in the Width area and 297mm in the Height area. Select the CMKY Color radio button, and then click OK. Choose File, Print Setup and select A3 from the Size drop-down list. Set the Direction to Vertical, and then click OK.

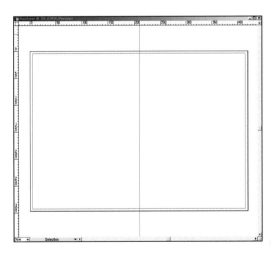

Step 2

Press Command/Ctrl + R to make a guide in the middle of the canvas to establish the Brochure's layout. This will make the ruler visible in the window. Click the left portion of the ruler and drag it to the middle of the canvas.

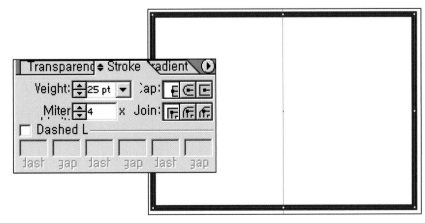

Step 3

Selecting the Rectangle tool, draw in a rectangle the size of the window. Set the Fill to None and the Stroke to black. In the Stroke palette, enter 25pt in the Weight area to create a black border around the canvas.

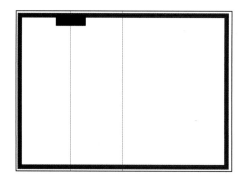

Step 4

Make the space for the title using the Rectangle tool, as shown here.

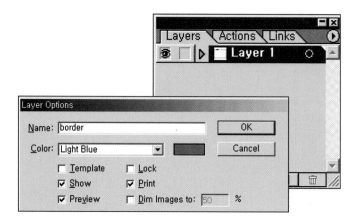

Step 5

Name Layer 1 "border."

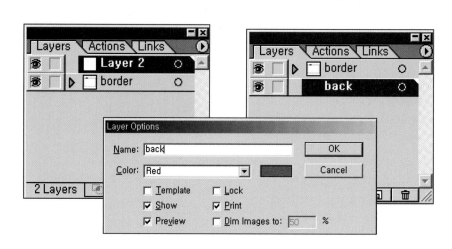

Step 6

Create a new layer and name it "back." Drag the back layer below the border layer.

Step 7

Make the back layer active and use the Pen tool to draw in the shape, as shown here, which will make up the background.

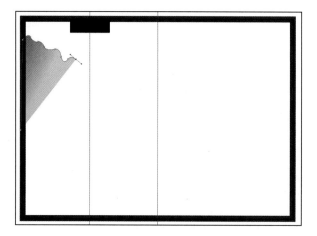
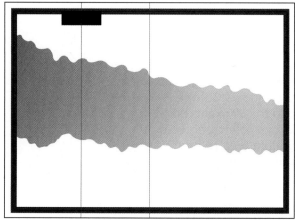

Step 8
Select this image by clicking on it while pressing the Command/Ctrl key. To use this image as a background image, set the Opacity to 25% in the Transparency palette.

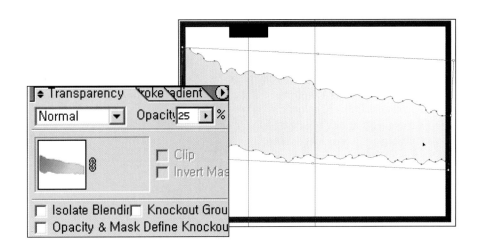

Step 9
In the Layers palette, drag the back layer, which contains the background image, onto the Create New Layer button to copy it. This will create a new back copy layer. Set the Opacity of this new layer to 50% in the Transparency palette.

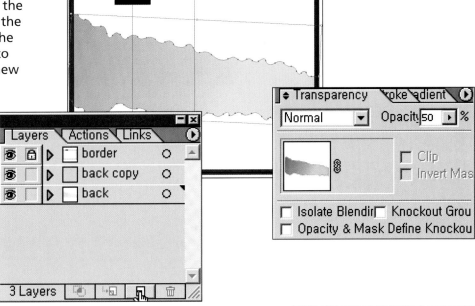

Step 10
Choose Effect, Blur, Radial Blur. In the Radial Blur dialog box enter 49 in the Amount area, select the Zoom and Good radio buttons.

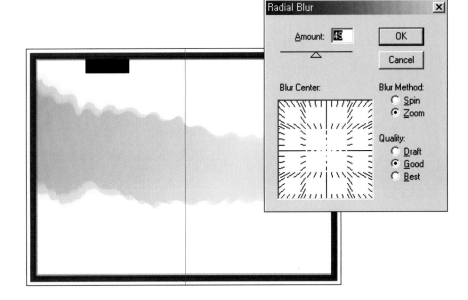

Step 11

Selecting the mural image in the wallpainting file, which we made previously (Command/Ctrl + A), copy (Command/Ctrl + C) and paste (Command/Ctrl +V) it on the Brochures canvas. Increasing it to an appropriate size, position it in the lower right-hand side of the canvas.

ELEMENT 6
Entering the Title and the Text Body

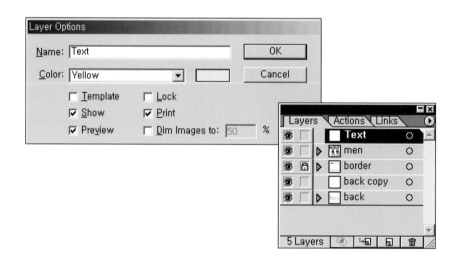

Step 1

Create a new layer button and name it "Text."

Step 2

Select the Type tool. To make the text white, set the Fill to white and the Stroke to None. Select the title line in the upper left-hand corner of the screen, type "Tourism."

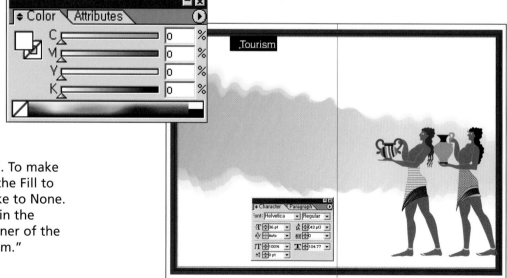

Step 3

Choose Window, Type, Character to open the Character palette (Command/Ctrl + T). Click and hold down the Command/Ctrl key on the word "Tourism" to set the Font to Monotype C and the Size to 36pt.

Step 4

Select the Type tool. Adjust the CMYK values for Fill to make a brick color. Select Trebuchet Ms from the Font pull-down list and set 50pt in the Size area in the Character palette. Type "Ancient Egypt," as shown here

Step 5

Copy and paste in text related to Egypt tourism or any document you wish, as shown here.

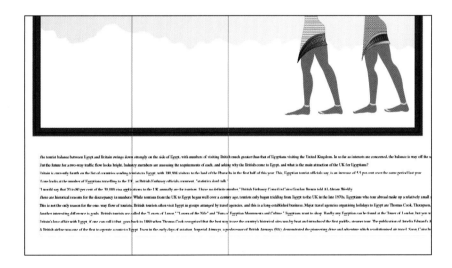

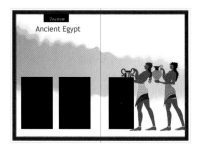

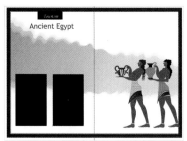

Step 6

Draw a rectangle to make a closed rectangular border for the text. Select the first rectangle while holding down the Command/Ctrl key, move it while pressing Option/Alt + Shift to copy it.

Step 7

To place the text inside the rectangle made in Step 6, select the Area Type tool. Click the upper left-hand corner of the rectangle where the text starts. An I-beam text cursor appears allowing you to enter text.

Step 8

Copy and paste the previously made text inside the rectangular box.

Step 9

We can see in the image that the text extends beyond the space allotted by the first rectangle. To make the text flow naturally into the adjacent boxes, select the Selection tool and press the Shift key, then click the adjacent boxes in which the text will continue.

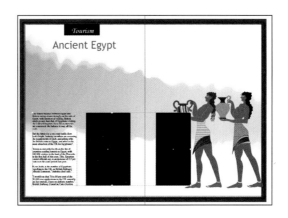

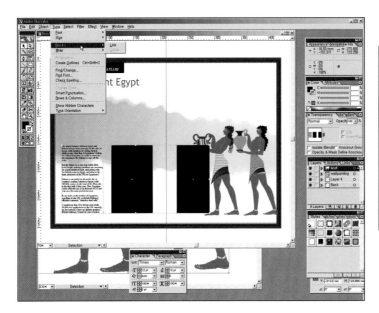

Step 10

Choose Type, Blocks, Link. This causes the text to flow naturally into the adjacent boxes.

Step 11

In the Character palette, set the Font to Times, the Size to 10pt, and the Line Spacing to 12pt.

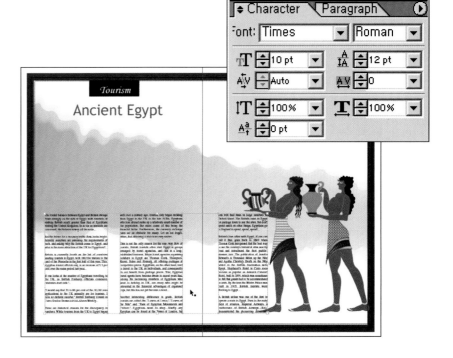

Step 12

Choose Window, Type, Paragraph (Command/Ctrl + M). Align the text by clicking on the Justify Full Lines in the Paragraph palette.

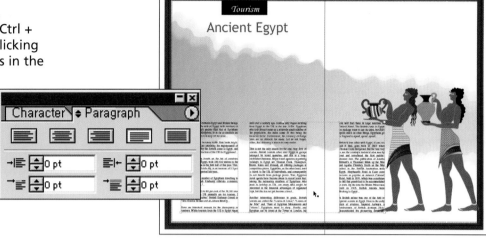

Step 13

Select the Type tool and enter the text shown here in the upper right-hand corner of the canvas. Press Enter to move to the next line.

Step 14

With the Type tool selected, click and drag the mouse on the text that you wish to emphasize.

Step 15

In the Character palette, set the Font to Helvetica and the Size to 14pt. Set the Fill color, as shown here, and the font color to a red.

Step 16

Select all of the text. Convert the selected text into an image by choosing Type, Create Outlines (Command/Ctrl + Shift + O). Converting the text to Create Outlines will prevent printing errors.

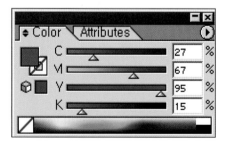

Step 17

Create a new layer and name it "images," click the OK button.

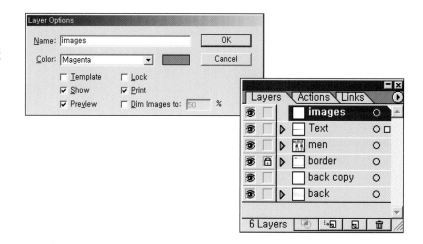

Step 18

Choose File, Place. In the Place dialog box, select the BOOK_10/PROJECT05/SOURCE/ PYRAMID.JPG file from the supplementary CD-ROM and then click the Place button to load the PYRAMID.JPG image.

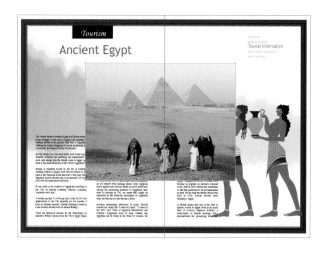

Step 19

Adjust the pyramid file to an appropriate size and position it, as shown here. The layout is now somewhat complete.

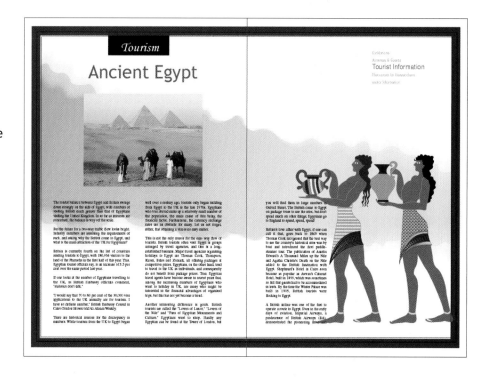

Step 20

Copy the vase held by the second man. When selecting the vase, hold down the Shift key to select all the elements that make up the vase.

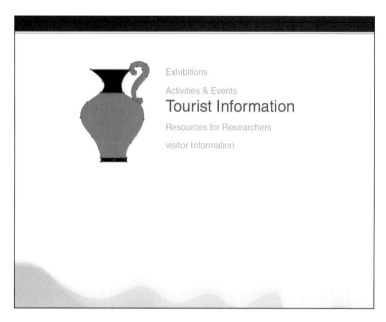

Step 21

Paste (Command/Ctrl + V) the vase as shown here. Double-click the Scale tool in the toolbox to open the Scale dialog box. Checking Preview, adjust the Scale value to reduce the icon to an appropriate size.

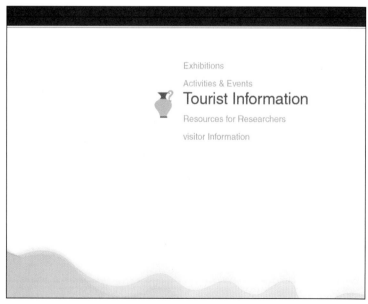

ELEMENT 7
Drawing a Map of Egypt

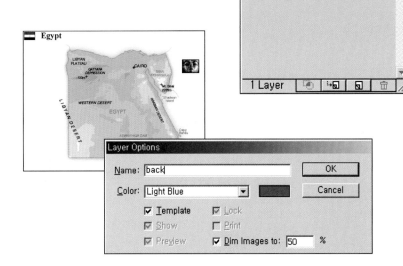

Step 1
Choose File, Open to load the BOOK_10/PROJECT05/SOURCE/ EG_MAP.JPG image. Name Layer 1 "back," and select the Template checkbox. This will convert the back layer into a template layer.

Step 2
The back image is now fixed on the template screen and will not be affected by any tool.

Step 3
Create a new layer and name it "map," click the OK button.

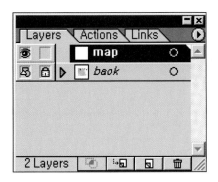

Step 4

Use the Pen tool to outline the map image.

Step 5

Select the entire map. Choose Effect, Stylize, Drop Shadow to open the Drop Shadow dialog box. In the Drop Shadow dialog box, select the Preview checkbox and Multiply from the Mode drop-down list. Set the Opacity to 75%, X Offset to 2mm, Y Offset to 2mm, Blur to 1.76mm, and then click OK to apply the effects.

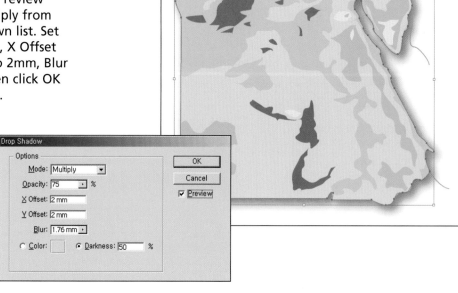

Step 6

Create a new layer and name it "text," click the OK button.

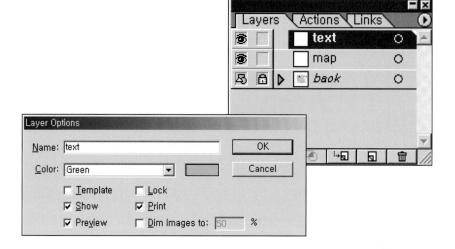

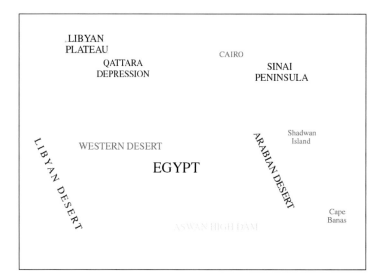

Step 7

Use the Type tool to enter the city names on the map, as shown here.

Step 8

Drag and drop the back layer into the trash. This completes the map image. To convert the text to images, choose Type, Create Outlines (Command/Ctrl + Shift + O).

Step 9

In order to emphasize the word "EGYPT," use the Type tool to click and select this text while holding down the Command/Ctrl key. Choose Type, Create Outlines to convert the text into an image. Set the Fill color to black and the Stroke to None.

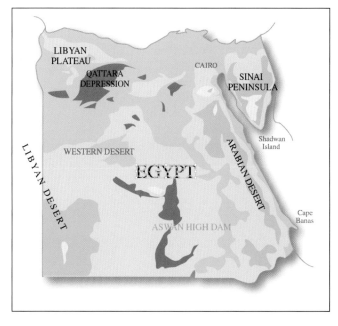

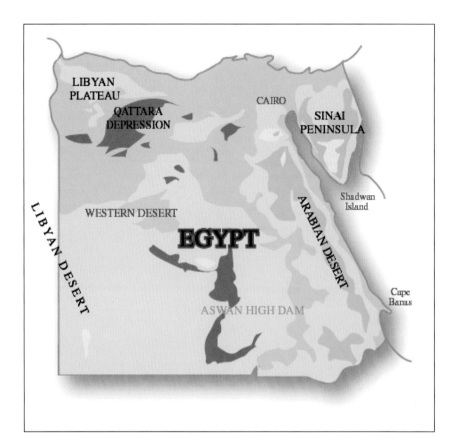

Step 10

Copy and Paste in Back to paste EGYPT (Command/Ctrl + B) slightly behind the text. Set the Weight to 3 in the Stroke palette and the Stroke color to red to create an outlined text.

Step 11

Select the entire map including the text. Copy and Paste the map into the brochure and position it accordingly in the upper right-hand side of the screen. If the image is too big, click the Scale tool to open the Scale dialog box and adjust the Scale to 70%.

Tourism

Ancient Egypt

Exhibitions

Activities & Events

Tourist Information

Resources for Researcher

Visitor Information

The tourist balance between Egypt and Britain swings down strongly on the side of Egypt, with numbers of visiting British much greater than that of Egyptians visiting the United Kingdom. In so far as interests are concerned, the balance is way off the scale.

But the future for a two-way traffic flow looks bright. Industry members are assessing the requirements of each, and asking why the British come to Egypt, and what is the main attraction of the UK for Egyptians?

Britain is currently fourth on the list of countries sending tourists to Egypt, with 180,904 visitors to the land of the Pharaohs in the first half of this year. This, Egyptian tourist officials say, is an increase of 5.5 per cent over the same period last year.

If one looks at the number of Egyptians travelling to the UK, as British Embassy officials comment, "statistics don't talk."

"I would say that 70 to 80 per cent of the 30,000 visa applications to the UK annually are for tourism. I have no definite number," British

Embassy Consul in Cairo Gordon Brown told Al-Ahram Weekly.

There are historical reasons for the discrepancy in numbers. While tourism from the UK to Egypt began well over a century ago, tourists only began trickling from Egypt to the UK in the late 1970s. Egyptians who tour abroad make up a relatively small number of the population, the main cause of this being the financial factor. Furthermore, the currency exchange rates are an obstacle for many. Let us not forget, either, that obtaining a visa is no easy matter.

This is not the only reason for the one-way flow of tourists. British tourists often visit Egypt in groups arranged by travel agencies, and this is a long-established business. Major travel agencies organising holidays to Egypt are Thomas Cook, Thompson, Kuoni, Bales and Zornack, all offering packages at competitive prices. Egyptians, on the other hand, tend to travel to the UK as individ-uals, and consequently do not benefit from package prices. True, Egyptian travel agents have become aware in recent years that, among the increasing numbers of Egyptians who want to holiday in UK, are many who might be interested

in the financial advantages of organised trips, but this has not yet become a trend.

Another interesting difference is goals. British tourists are called the "Lovers of Luxor," "Lovers of the Nile" and "Fans of Egyptian Monuments and Culture." Egyptians want to shop. Hardly any Egypt-ian can be found at the Tower of London, but you will find them in large numbers in Oxford Street. The British come to Egypt on package tours to see the sites, but don't spend much on other things. Egyptians go to England to spend, spend, spend!

Britain's love affair with Egypt, if one can call it that, goes back to 1869 when Thomas Cook recognis-ed that the best way to see the country's historical sites was by boat and introduced the first paddle- steamer tour. The publication of Amelia Edward's A

Project 6
Tarot Card Design

PROJECT 6
Tarot Card Design

Repeating objects are created easily using Copy, Reflect, Rotate, and Shear tools. You will use bitmap image filters and effects to create a unique tarot card design.

Source Files

Painting.jpg

Frame.jpg

ELEMENT 1
Drawing the Background of the Tarot Cards

Step 1
Open a new document (Command/Ctrl + N) and name it "Tarot card." Select Custom from the Size drop-down list and Centimeters from the Units drop-down list. Set the Width to 7cm and Height to 12cm. Select the CMYK Color radio button, and then click OK.

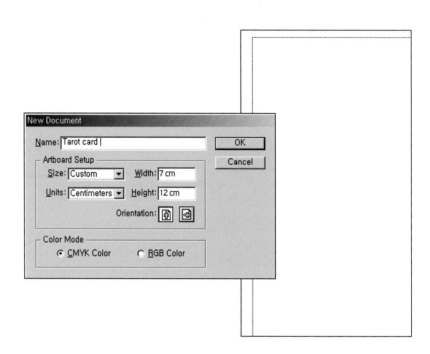

Step 2
Choose View, Hide Page Tiling so that the page lines do not show. Rename Layer 1 "background," and then click OK.

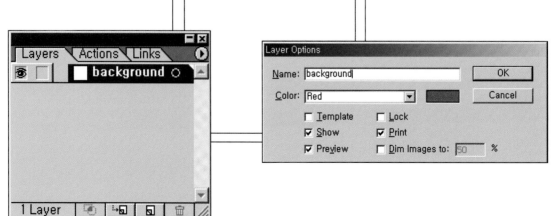

Step 3

In the Color palette, set the Fill color to a light yellow and the Stroke color to black. In the Stroke palette, select 0.25pt from the Weight drop-down list.

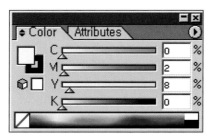

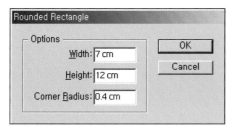

Step 4

Select the Rounded Rectangle tool and click an empty space on the screen to open the Rounded Rectangle dialog box. In the Rounded Rectangle dialog box, set the Width to 7cm, Height to 12cm, and Corner Radius to 0.4cm, and then click OK. Selecting a tool, such as the Selection or Direct Selection tool, or clicking on an empty space on the canvas while pressing the Command/Ctrl key will show the rectangle in its unselected state.

Step 5

Choose View, Hide Artboard to hide the canvas lines from the screen.

ELEMENT 2
Adding Guides and Drawing Decorative Images

Step 1

Choose File, Place. In the Place dialog box, select the BOOK_10/PROJECT06/SOURCE/FRAME.JPG file from the supplementary CD-ROM and select the Template checkbox. Look at the Layers palette, you can see that you already made the template layer.

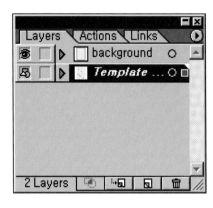

Step 2

Select the Scale tool and size it to fit the background of the tarot card. In the Color palette, click the Transparency tab and set the Opacity to 43% so that the tarot card background appears subtle.

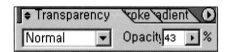

Step 3

Deselect the image. Create a new layer and name it "pattern1." Choose View, Show Rulers.

Step 4

Click and drag the top left-hand corner of the ruler to the edge of the tarot card. This will convert the position of the 0 on the ruler to the left alignment of the tarot card.

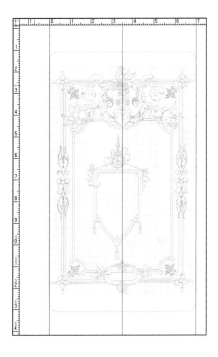

Step 5

Lock the guides by Choosing View, Guides, Lock Guides (Command/Ctrl + Option/Alt + ;). A checkmark next to Lock Guides indicates that the guides are locked. Locking the guides is very convenient as it prevents the object from being selected twice. Outline the image on the template screen using the Pen tool.

Step 6

Set the Fill to None. Complete one element, as shown here. Set the Stroke color to red in order to differentiate between the template and your outline.

Step 7

Use the Pen tool to outline the image of the column, as shown here.

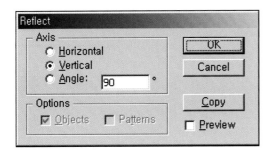

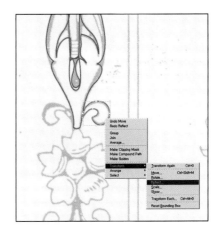

Step 8

Select one side of the decorative ornament. Right-click (Command + Click) and select Transform, Reflect. In the Reflect dialog box, select the Vertical radio button and set the Angle to 90°. Click Copy. A symmetrical copy will appear along the vertical axis.

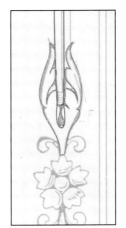

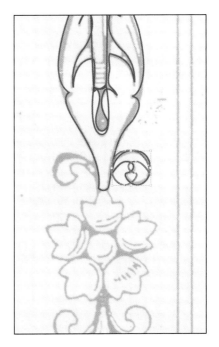

Step 9

Move the copied ornament to the left. Hold the Shift key as you do so, and the ornament will move along the horizontal axis.

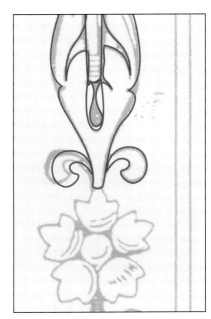

ELEMENT 3
Drawing Flowers Using the Rotate Tool

Step 1

Use the Pen tool to outline one flower petal. Use the Rotate tool to arrange the central axis in the middle of the flower. Click and rotate the completed flower petal clockwise. To duplicate the flower petal, hold down the Option/Alt key while doing this.

Step 2

Press Command/Ctrl + D to duplicate the flower petal in the angle that they were copied. Duplicate the remaining flower petals using Command/Ctrl + D.

Step 3

Select the Ellipse tool to draw the center of the flower.

Step 4
Select the entire flower object. Right-click (Command + Click) and select Group to group together the six individual elements.

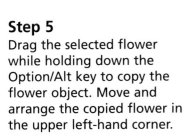

Step 5
Drag the selected flower while holding down the Option/Alt key to copy the flower object. Move and arrange the copied flower in the upper left-hand corner.

ELEMENT 4
Adding Color to Objects Using the Gradient and Brush

Step 1

Use the Pen tool to draw the decorative ornament shown here.

Step 2

Select the bar element shown here. Click the Gradient button in the color mode to make the Fill color a gradient. In the Gradient palette, click the Color tab and in the Color palette, click the Option button and select CMYK. This allows us to establish the color. Use the Gradient tool and drag in many different directions until the desired effect is achieved.

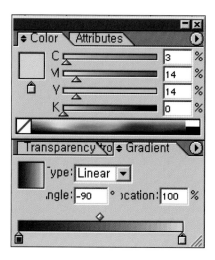

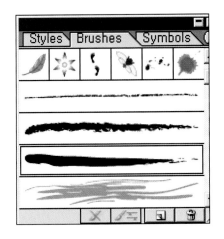

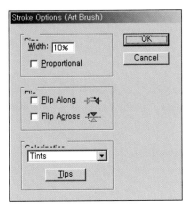

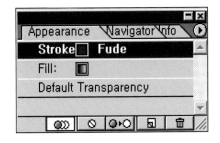

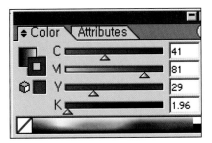

Step 3

Choose Window, Brushes to open the Brushes palette (F5). Set the Stroke color shown here. Then, click the Art Brushes brush in the Brushes palette and apply it to the Stroke. Reduce the size of the brush by choosing Window, Appearance (Shift + F6). In the Appearance dialog box, double-click Stroke and in the Stroke Options dialog box, set the Width to 10%, and then click OK. Art Brushes has now been applied to the Stroke of the image.

Step 4

Select the vertical bar shown here. Click the Eyedropper tool on the horizontal bar for which the gradient has already been applied. This gradient will appear in the vertical bar.

Step 5

Apply the Gradient tool until the desired result is achieved. You can exit from the Gradient tool by pressing the Command/Ctrl key and clicking an empty space on the canvas.

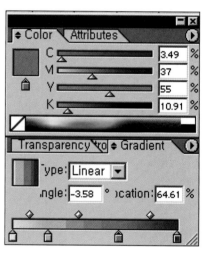

Step 6

Select a decorative ornament. Click the Eyedropper tool on the bar to apply the same gradient to the decorative ornament. Click the Color tab in the Gradient palette and establish the color in the Color palette. Apply the Gradient tool in different directions until the desired result is achieved.

Step 7

Set the Stroke color shown here. Select Art Brushes in the Brushes palette. You can see that the Stroke is too large as compared to the ornament. Double-click Stroke in the Appearance palette to open the Stroke Options dialog box. In the Stroke Options dialog box, set the Width to 10%, and then click OK.

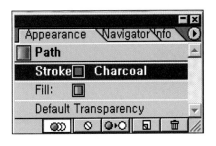

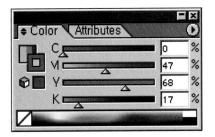

Step 8

Select another decorative ornament. Click the Eyedropper tool on the previous ornament to apply the same gradient. In the Gradient palette, set the Type to Radial and then apply the Gradient tool until the desired result is achieved. Select another ornament and fill it in with the gradient color.

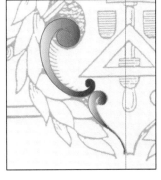

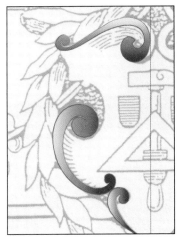

ELEMENT 5
Making Flower Objects

Step 1

Select the flower shown here. Undo the grouping by right-clicking (Command + Click) on the flower and selecting Ungroup. Click the Color tab in the Gradient palette and establish the color in the Color palette. Apply the Gradient tool until the desired result is achieved.

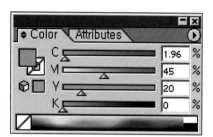

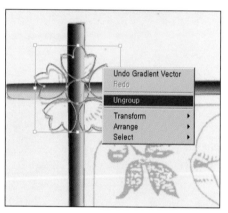

Step 2

Establish the Stroke color in the Color palette and select Art Brushes in the Brushes palette. Double-click Stroke in the Appearance palette to open the Stroke Options dialog box. In the Stroke Options dialog box, set the Width to 3%, and then click OK.

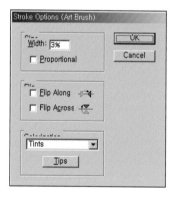

Step 3

Select the flower petal. Click the Eyedropper tool on the flower to apply the same gradient and brush effect to the flower petal. Apply the Gradient tool until the desired result is achieved. Repeat this step until you have completed the flower.

Step 4

Select each of the flower petals until they are all selected. Right-click (Command + Click) and select Group to group them together.

Step 5

Copy the flower. To move the flower vertically, hold down the Shift key. Using the Rotate tool, rotate the flower, as shown here.

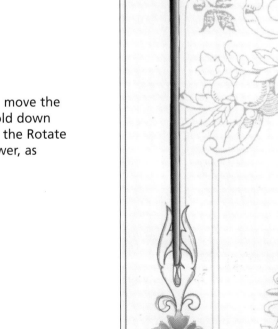

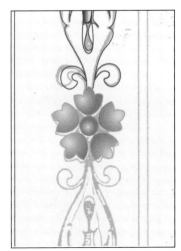

ELEMENT 6
Simplifying Complex Objects Using the Reflect Tool

Step 1

Select the ornamental element shown here. Click the Eyedropper tool on the flower petal for which the gradient has already been established to apply the same gradient and brush effect to the selected ornamental element. Apply the Gradient tool until the desired result is achieved. Repeat this step until the ornamental element is complete.

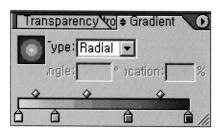

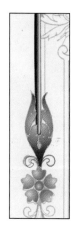

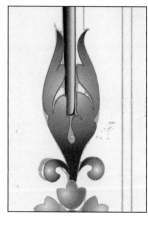

Step 2

Choose View, Outline so that the lines of the artwork are visible (Command/Ctrl + Y). Objects that are difficult to select can be selected easily in Outline format. Select View, Preview to go back to the artwork.

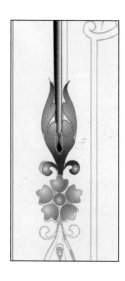

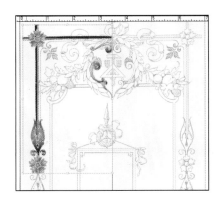
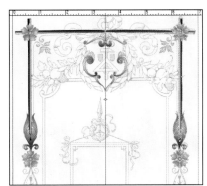

Step 3

Select the entire image, as shown here. Use the Reflect tool to bring the central axis to the middle. Hold down the Option/Alt key and drag the image in the desired direction to make a copy. This will make a symmetrical copy of the object.

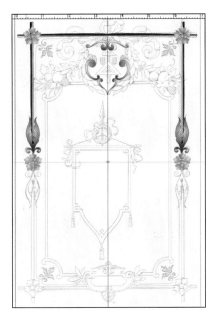

Step 4

Click the ruler and drag to the middle to make a horizontal guide. Drag the Selection tool around the image, excluding the flowers at the bottom to select it, as shown here. Use the Reflect tool to bring the central axis to the middle. Hold down the Option/Alt key and drag the object in the desired direction to make a copy. This will make a symmetrical copy, as shown.

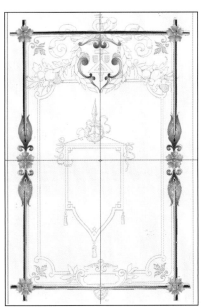

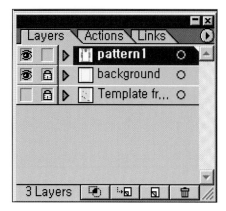

Step 5

Hide the Template layer in the Layers palette. After your work is finished you can delete this Template layer by dragging and dropping on the Delete Selection icon.

ELEMENT 7
Making the Decorative Text and Petals

Step 1

Create a new layer button and name it "pattern2." Lock all the layers excluding the pattern2 layer. You lock the layers to prevent them from being selected when working in another layer, which will make your work more efficient. Use the Pen tool to draw the decorative ornament shown here. Choose View, Show Rulers to see the ruler.

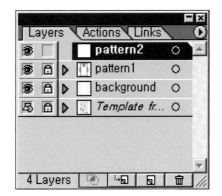

Step 2

Use the Pen tool to draw the leaves, as shown here.

Step 3

Select the decorative ornament. Click the Eyedropper tool on the gradient shown here to apply it to the selected ornament. In the Gradient palette, select Radial from the Type pull-down list, and then apply the Gradient tool until the desired result is achieved. Select another ornament and fill it with the gradient color.

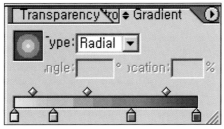

Step 4

Select the leaf. Click the Eyedropper tool on the object, for which the gradient has already been established, to apply the same gradient to the leaf. In the Gradient palette, click the Color tab and set the color in the Color palette. Then, select Radial from the Type pull-down list, and then apply the Gradient tool until the desired result is achieved. Select another leaf and fill it with the gradient color. Change the Stroke color in the Color palette to the color of the leaf shown here.

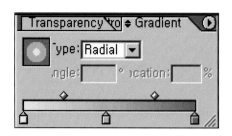

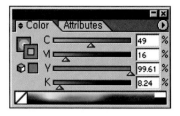

ELEMENT 8
Drawing a Pretty Ribbon Using the Gradient Tool

Step 1

Use the Pen tool to outline the sketch ribbon. In the Gradient palette, click the Color tab and establish the color in the Color palette. Select Radial from the Type pull-down list, and then apply the Gradient tool until the desired result is achieved.

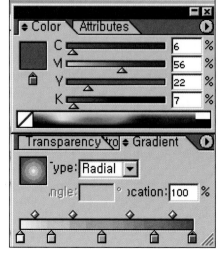

Step 2

Change the Stroke color in the Color palette to the color of the ribbon seen here.

Step 3

Send one surface of the ribbon to the back so that it does not overlap with the bar. Use the Scissors tool to select the portion of the ribbon that will be cut out, and then press the Del key.

ELEMENT 9
Making the Decorative Petal Object

Step 1

Hide the pattern1 layer. Use the Pen tool to complete the decorative leaf.

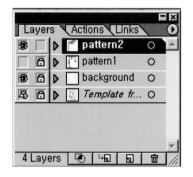

Step 2

Make the pattern1 layer visible again. Use the Pen tool to complete the decorative leaf.

Step 3
Select all of the leaves. Using the Eyedropper tool apply the same gradient that you used with the other leaves to these leaves.

Step 4

Select the leaves. In the Gradient palette, select Linear from the Type drop-down list, and then apply the Gradient tool until the desired result is achieved. Change the brightness of the color for each leaf to create a natural result.

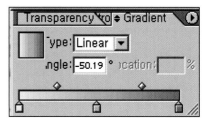

Step 5

Change the image's position by selecting it and then right-clicking (Command + Click) to select Arrange, Bring to Front (Command/Ctrl + Shift +]).

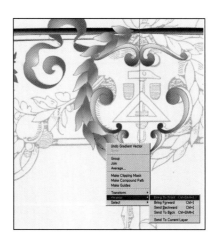

Step 6

Change the position of another leaf by selecting it and then right-clicking (Command + Click) to select Arrange, Send to Back (Command/Ctrl + Shift + [).

ELEMENT 10
Making a Natural Decorative Petal

Step 1

Use the Pen tool to draw in the remaining leaves.

Step 2

Select all the elements shown here. Click the Eyedropper tool on the previous leaves to apply the same gradient to the selected ones here.

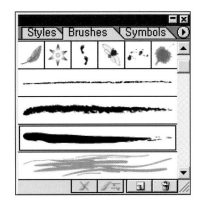

Step 3

Select the stem object, as shown here. Select Air Brush from the Brushes palette. Double-click the brush to open the Art Brush Options dialog box and set the Width to 3%, and click OK.

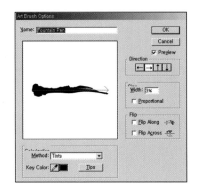

Step 4

Change the position of the leaf by selecting it and then right-clicking (Command + Click) to select Arrange, Bring to Front (Command/Ctrl + Shift +]). Change the position of another leaf by selecting it and then right-clicking (Command + Click) to select Arrange, Send to Back (Command/Ctrl + Shift + [).

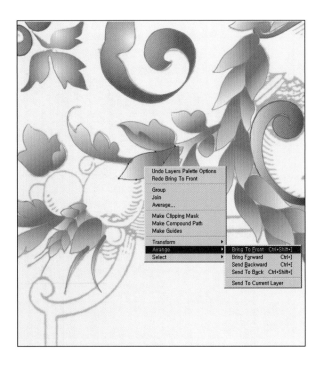

Step 5

Create a more natural leaf by clicking on the Color tab in the Gradient palette, and then adjusting the color in the Color palette.

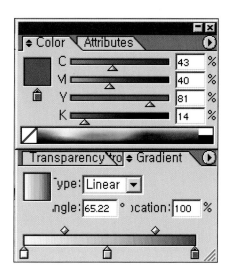

ELEMENT 11
Adding Dimensionality Using the Gradient Mesh Tool

Step 1
Create a new layer and name it "pattern3." Use the Pen tool to draw the fruit.

Step 2
Draw round fruit using the Ellipse tool. Set the Fill color shown here.

Step 3
Use the Mesh tool to create a mesh point. Set the color in the Color palette and then click to create a mesh point. Click the point before establishing the color. You can also move the points by dragging them with the mouse. Change the position and color of the points until the desired effect is achieved.

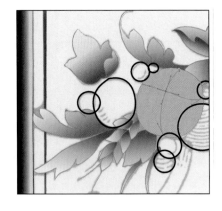

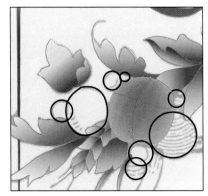

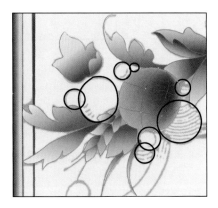

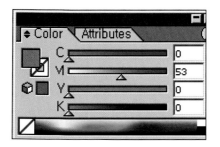

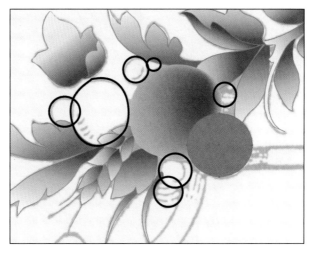

Step 4

Similarly, select the fruit and use the Mesh tool to add dimensionality.

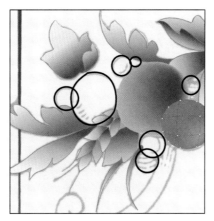
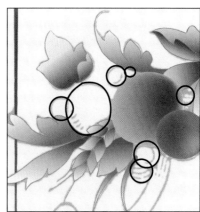

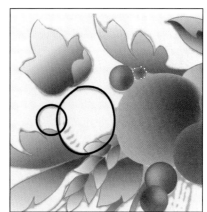

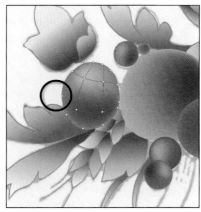

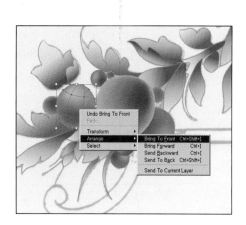

Step 5

To change the fruit's position, right-click (Command + Click) to select Arrange, Bring to Front (Command/Ctrl + Shift +]). Change the position of another fruit.

ELEMENT 12
Making Symmetrical Objects Using the Reflect Tool

Step 1

Click the pattern2 layer in the Layers palette and select the decorative leaf element, as shown here. Right-click (Command + Click) and select Group to group the elements together.

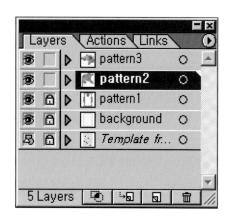

Step 2

Use the Reflect tool to bring the central axis to the guide in the middle. Hold down the Option/Alt key and drag the image to make a copy. Holding down the Shift key will make a symmetrical copy of the object.

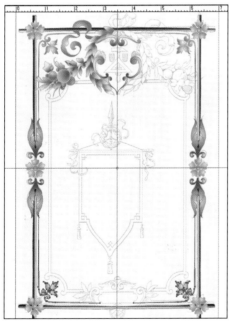

Step 3

Select the decorative elements at the top, as shown here. Use the Reflect tool to bring the central axis to the guide in the middle. Hold down the Option/Alt key and drag the elements to make a copy.

Step 4

Select all the leaves, as shown here. Right-click (Command + Click) and group the selected elements together. Select the fruit and ribbon as well.

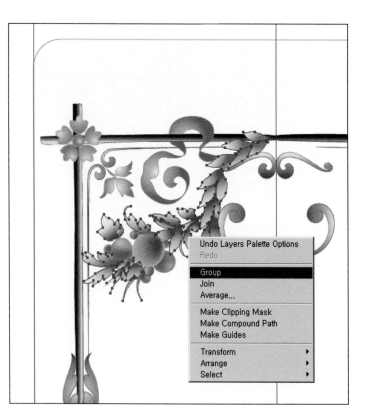

Step 05

Use the Reflect tool to bring the central axis to the guide in the middle. Hold down the Option/Alt key and drag the image to make a copy.

ELEMENT 13
Making Decorative Objects

Step 1

Use the Pen tool to draw the ribbon shown here. Click the Eyedropper tool on the ribbon you drew earlier to apply the same gradient. Then, apply the Gradient tool until the desired result is achieved.

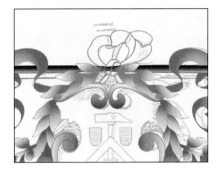
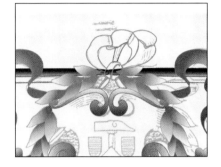

Step 2

Place the decorative element over the leaf by moving the pattern1 layer over the pattern2 layer in the Layers palette. Select the decorative element using the Selection tool and right-click (Command + Click) to select Arrange, Bring to Front (Command/Ctrl + Shift +]).

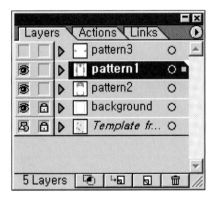

Step 3

Create a new layer and name it "pattern4." Then use the Pen tool to draw in the inner lines shown here.

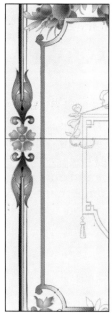
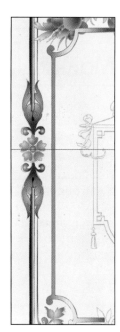

Step 4

Select the line and use the Reflect tool to bring the central axis to the middle. Hold down the Option/Alt key and drag the line to make a copy. Holding down the Shift key will make a symmetrical copy of the line.

Step 5

Move the pattern4 layer above the pattern1 layer in the Layers palette. Select the line and right-click (Command + Click) to select Arrange, Send To Back (Command/Ctrl + Shift + [).

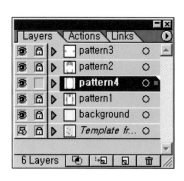

Step 6

Create a new layer and name it "pattern5." Then use the Pen tool to draw in the decorative lines at the bottom.

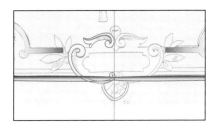

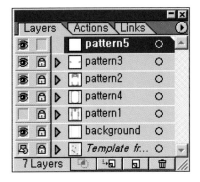

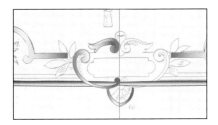

Step 7

Select the line and use the Reflect tool to bring the central axis to the middle. Hold down the Option/Alt key and drag the line to make a copy. Holding down the Shift key will make a symmetrical copy of the object.

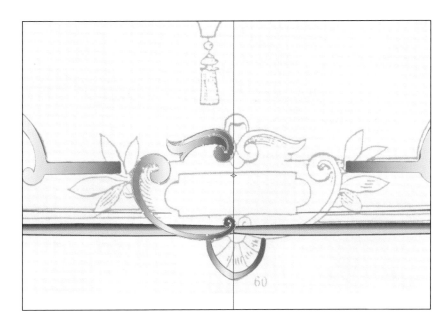

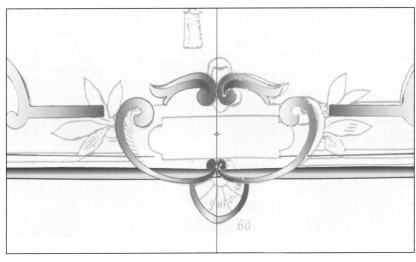

Step 8

Use the Pen and Eyedropper tools to complete the leaf. Use the Reflect tool to bring the central axis to the middle. Hold down the Option/Alt key and drag the leaf to make a copy. Holding down the Shift key will make a symmetrical copy of the leaf.

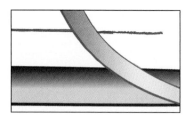

Step 9

Click and drag the Scissors tool over the portion of the line you want to cut out. Select the cut line and press the Del key. In the Layers palette, drag and drop the Template layer over the Delete Selection icon.

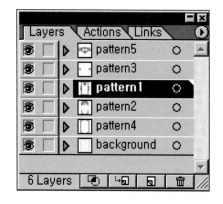

ELEMENT 14
Entering Text in the Tarot Card

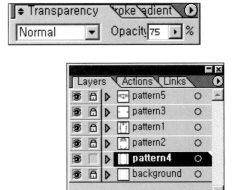

Step 1

Select the pattern4 layer in the Layers palette. In the Transparency palette, set the Opacity to 75%.

Step 2

Select the pattern2 layer. Right-click (Command + Click) and select Group to group the elements together. Then, in the Transparency palette, set the Opacity to 75%.

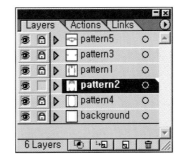

Step 3

Select the other layers, group them, and set the Opacity to 75% in the Transparency palette.

Step 4

Create a new layer and name it "text." Select the Type tool and enter the words "THE WORLD OF FORTUNE" at the bottom of the tarot card. Choose Window, Type, Character to open the Character palette (Command/Ctrl + T). In the Character palette, adjust the font, font size and spacing, as shown here. The font and font size can also be adjusted by selecting Type, Font, Size.

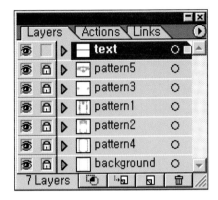

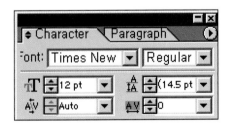

Step 5

Use the Type tool to enter the Roman numerals VII. Establish the font and font size in the Character palette.

Step 6

Use the Type tool to enter the words "WANDS BATONS" at the top left-hand corner of the tarot card. Double-click Fill in the color mode to reveal the Color Picker dialog box. Set the color to red and then click OK. Then, establish the font and font size in the Character palette. The font and font size can also be adjusted by selecting Type, Font, Size.

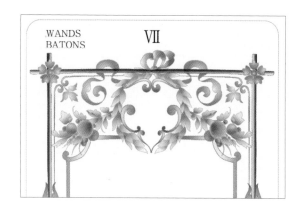

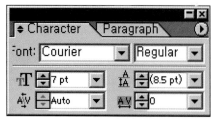

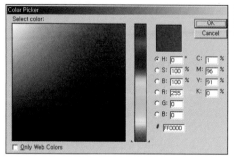

Step 7

Use the Type tool to enter the words "STAVE BASTOS" in the top right-hand corner of the tarot card. Click the Paragraph tab in the Character palette to open the Paragraph palette and then click the Align Right button to align the text to the right.

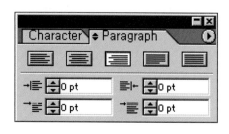

Step 8

Align the text, as shown here.
Select the text and align it to
the guide. You can also align
several different objects to
the same place using the
Align palette.

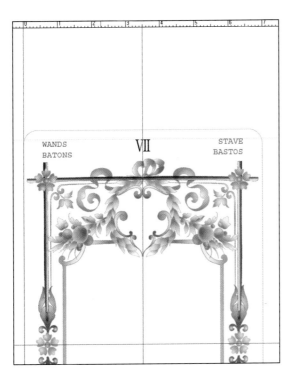

Step 9

We can see that the text at
the bottom of the tarot card
is large in proportion to the
tarot card. Select THE WORLD
OF FORTUNE text using the
Selection tool and reduce
the font size.

Step 10

Select the pattern1 layer in the Layers palette and select the bar object using the Selection tool. Right-click (Command + Click) and select Arrange, Send To Back (Command/Ctrl + Shift + []).

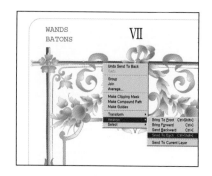

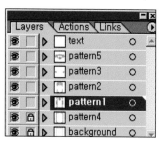

ELEMENT 15
Applying Filters to Masterpieces

Step 1

Choose File, Place the BOOK_10/PROJECT06/SOURCE/ PAINTING.JPG file from the supplementary CD-ROM.

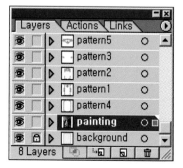

Step 2

Create a new layer and name it "painting." Place it right above the background layer. Use the Selection tool to arrange the PAINTING.JPG image in the middle of the tarot card. We can see that the PAINTING.JPG image is too large, so make it smaller using the Scale tool. Pressing the Shift and Option/Alt keys while reducing the size will reduce the image proportionally..

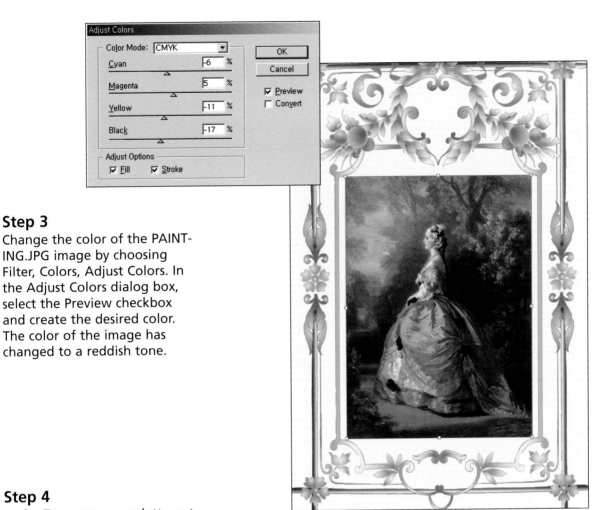

Step 3

Change the color of the PAINT-ING.JPG image by choosing Filter, Colors, Adjust Colors. In the Adjust Colors dialog box, select the Preview checkbox and create the desired color. The color of the image has changed to a reddish tone.

Step 4

In the Transparency palette, set the Blending Mode to Luminosity and the Opacity to 80%. This causes the image to fade slightly.

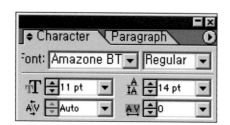

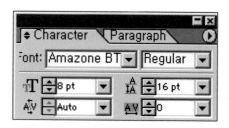

Step 5

Use the Type tool to enter the words "WANDS BATONS," as shown here. Adjust the font, font size and spacing in the Character palette. Enter the text "Stave Bastons," as shown here and adjust the font, font size and spacing.

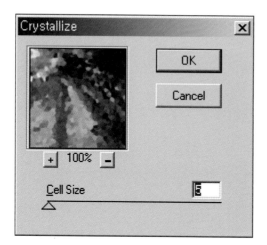

Step 6

Use the Selection tool to select the painting and choose Effect, Pixelate, Crystallize. In the Crystallize dialog box, set the Cell Size to 5 and then click OK. You have now completed the Tarot card.

WANDS
BATONS

VII

STAVE
BASTOS

Wands
Batons

Stave Bastons

THE WORLD OF FORTUNE

Project 7
Time of EGYPT

2002 EGYPT

Time of EGPYT

PROJECT 7
Time of EGYPT

Illustrator is most often used to create precise and simplified images. After using the Blend feature to draw the frame of a postage stamp, you will use Illustrator's Transform tool to complete the image of the compass. This simple postage stamp is designed using an Egyptian theme.

Source Files

Pharoah.jpg

ELEMENT 1
Drawing the Outline of the Stamp Using Blend

Step 1

Choose File, New to open the New Document (Command/Ctrl + N). In the Name area type Stamp_border. Set the Size to A4, Width to 297mm, Height to 210mm, and select the CMYK Color radio button.

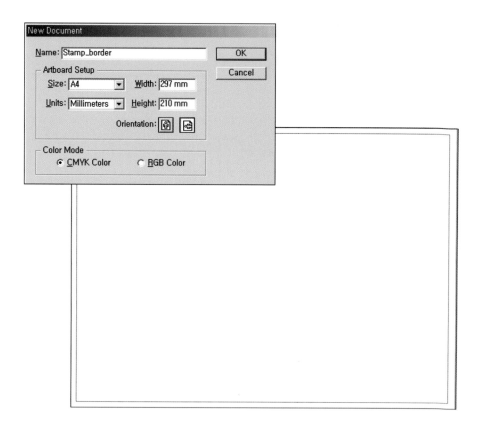

Step 2

Select the Rectangle tool to draw the outline of the stamp. In the Rectangle dialog box, set both the Width and Height to 150mm and click OK. A square will appear on the screen.

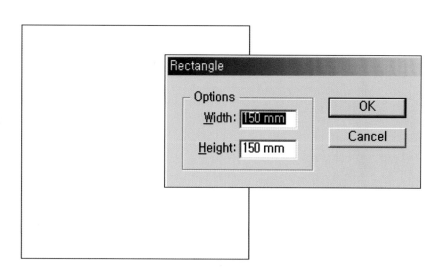

Step 3

You will now create a hollow circle in all four corners of the square. Select the Ellipse tool, hold down the Option/Alt key, and click precisely on the top left-hand corner of the square to make a circle that is centered on this corner.

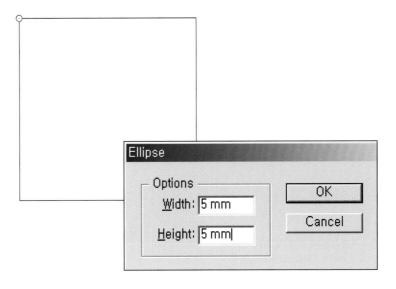

Step 4

Click and drag the completed circle to the bottom left-hand corner while holding down Shift+Option/Alt to make a copy of the circle.

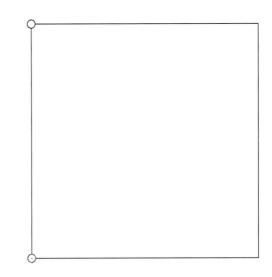

Step 5

Repeat Step 4 to copy the two circles onto the two right-hand corners.

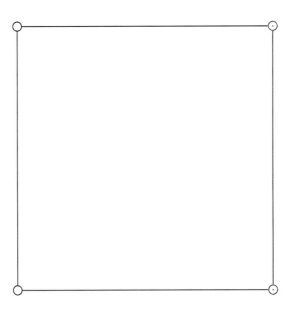

Step 6

You will now try using the Blend feature to make all four circles the same size. Select the circle on the top, left-hand corner and bottom, left-hand corner.

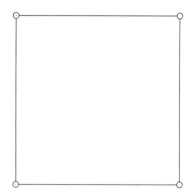

Step 7

You will now add 17 circles in between these two selected circles. Choose Object, Blend, Blend Options... from the menu bar. In the Blend Options dialog box, select Specified Steps from the Spacing drop-down list and enter 17.

Step 8

With the two circles selected, choose Object, Blend, Make (Command/Ctrl + Option/Alt + B) to create the 17 identical circles.

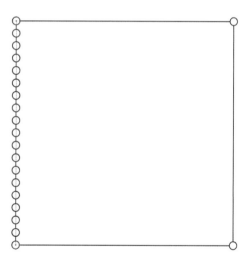

Step 9

The circles created in Step 8 used the original two circles as a source and are grouped together. Ungroup the circles. Choose Object, Blend, Release (Command/Ctrl + Shift + Option/Alt + B) to ungroup the blended circles. You now have 19 individual circles.

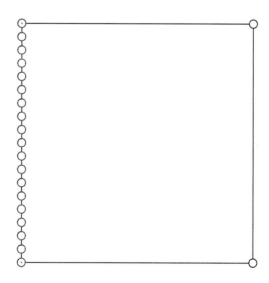

Step 10

Repeat Steps 7-9 to fill in the remaining sides with circles, which will be the stamp border for the completed image.

Step 11

Click and drag while holding down the Command/Ctrl key to select all the elements.

Step 12

Make the border for the stamp by choosing Window, Pathfinder to open the Pathfinder palette. Click the Subtract from shape area button under Shape Modes. You can see that the rectangular shape on the bottom is cut out.

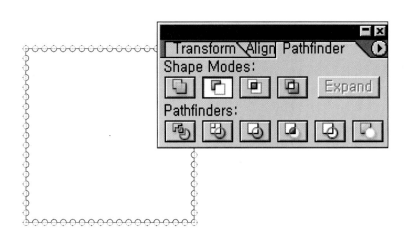

Step 13

Use the Expand button in the Pathfinder palette to remove the remaining traces of the circle to leave behind only a semi-circle, as shown here.

ELEMENT 2
Drawing the Pharaoh Background

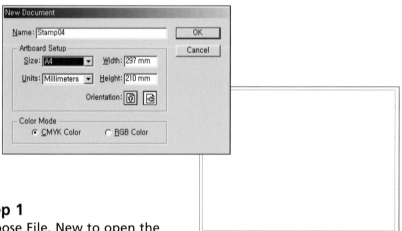

Step 1

Choose File, New to open the New Document dialog box (Command/Ctrl + N). In the Name area type "Stamp04," select A4 from the Size pull-down list, set the Width to 297mm, Height to 210mm, and select the CMYK Color radio button.

Step 2

Copy the border that you made in the Stamp_border file to the Stamp04 file.

Step 3

Choose Window, Attributes to open the Attributes panel (F11). Select the Show Center button to find the center point of the stamp border.

Step 4

Make the ruler visible by choosing View, Show Rulers. Click the ruler and drag the mouse to the center point to create a guide.

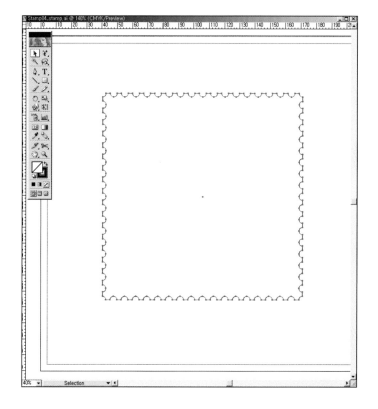

Step 5

Rename layer 1 in the Layers palette "border."

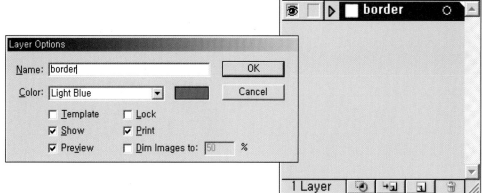

Step 6
Set the Fill color as shown here.

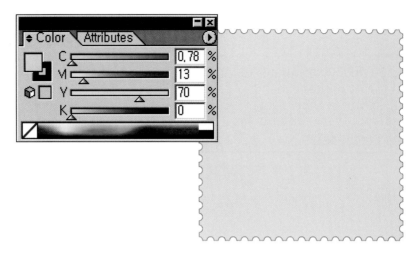

Step 7
Create a new layer and name it "image."

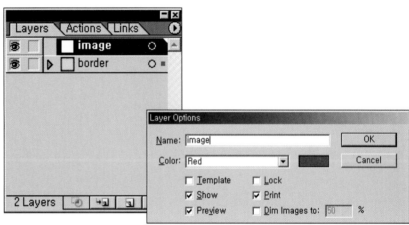

Step 8
Choose File, Place to load the BOOK_10/PROJECT07/SOURCE/ PHARAOH.JPG file from the supplementary CD-ROM.

Step 9

Choose Window, Transparency to open the Transparency palette and set the Opacity to 17% to create a natural blending of the image and the golden background color.

Step 10

Expand the size of the Pharaoh image to fit the size of the stamp border. Select the image while holding down the Command/Ctrl key and double-click the Scale button in the toolbox to open the Scale dialog box. Then, set the Uniform Scale to 122%, and click OK. Select the stamp border and set the Stroke to None.

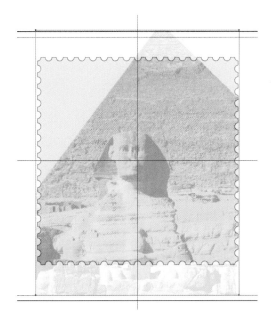

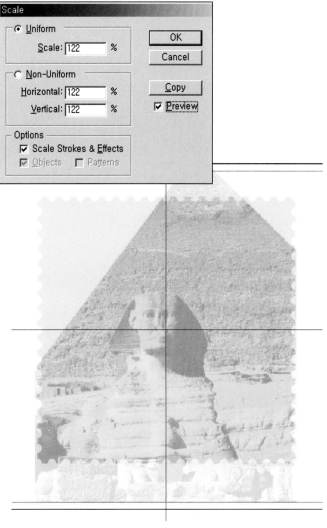

Step 11

Use the Clipping Mask function to remove the images that extend beyond the stamp border. In the Layers palette, drag the border layer onto the Create New Layer icon to make the border copy layer. Click and drag on the border copy layer and move it onto the image layer.

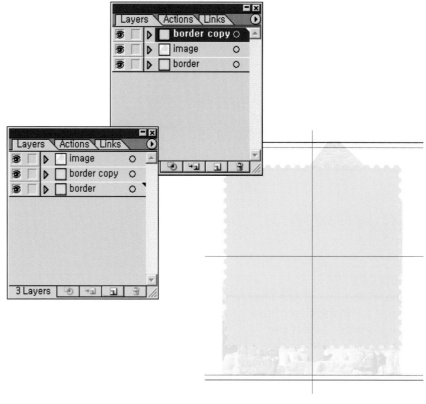

Step 12

Select the entire image.

Step 13

Choose Object, Clipping Mask, Make (Command/Ctrl + 7). The topmost object acts as the mask to hide the areas that extend beyond the border.

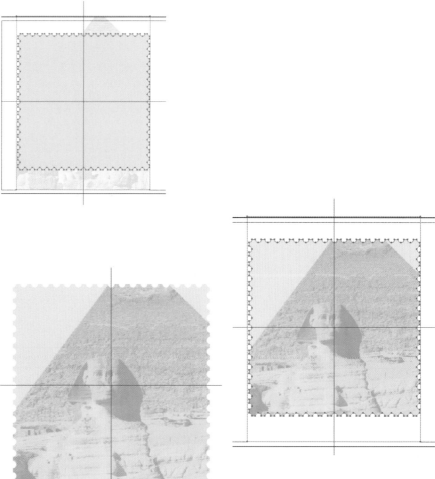

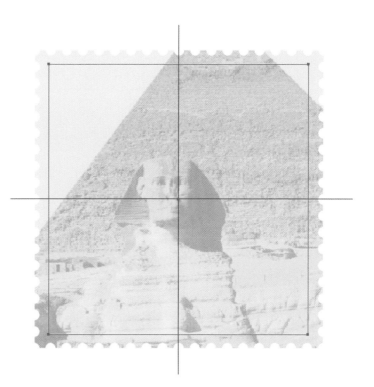

Step 14

Choose the Rectangle tool, click and drag on the center of the guide (created at the center of the object) while holding down the Option/Alt key to make a rectangular frame in the stamp. (Holding down the Shift key will create a square frame.)

ELEMENT 3
Making the Compass Using the Rotate Tool

Step 1
Create a new layer and name it "text1."

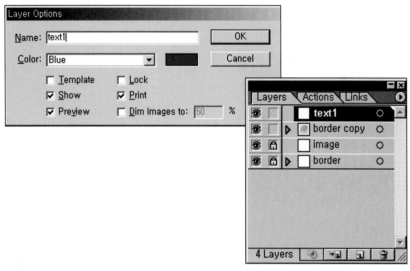

Step 2
Select the Ellipse tool while holding down Shift + Option/Alt to draw the compass. Choose View, Guides, Make Guides to convert the circle into a guide (Command/Ctrl + 5).

Step 3
Select the Pen tool to draw the direction lines of the compass.

Step 4

Select the Rotate tool so that the direction lines are evenly spaced all around the circle. Make the center guide the center by clicking on the center guide while holding down the Option/Alt key to open the Rotate dialog box. Set the Angle value to 3.8° and then press the Copy button. The line that we drew against the center guide is copied 3.8 degrees to the left.

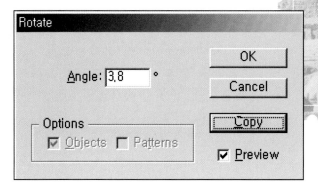

Step 5

Choose Object, Transform, Transform Again (Command/Ctrl + D). Continue to press Command/Ctrl + D to draw in direction lines, at 3.8 degree intervals, all around the circle.

Step 6

We want each line at every 20°
interval to be darkened. To do
so, use the Selection tool and
hold down the Shift key to
select all four direction lines,
excluding the very first line. In
the same way, leaving behind
one line, press the Shift key to
select the next four lines. This
will allow us to select all the
lines that will be created using
a thin line.

Step 7

Choose Window, Stroke (F10)
to open the Stroke palette. Set
the Weight to 0.5, and then
press Enter. This will apply a
0.5pt weight to the lines we
selected in Step 6.

Step 8

Now select the Type tool to
add in numbers to the compass.
Clicking the topmost line of
the compass enter 0. Press
Command/Ctrl + T to open the
Character palette and set the
Font to Times New Roman, the
Size to 5pt, and then press Enter.

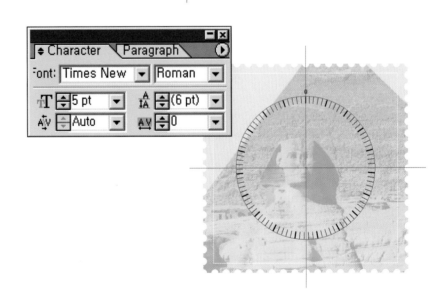

Step 9

We want the angle marks to appear evenly around the compass. To do so, select the Rotate tool and then click the center of the guide while holding down the Option/Alt key to open the Rotate dialog box. Set the Angle to 18.95°, and then press the Copy button. The number is now copied in 18.95° increments around the compass.

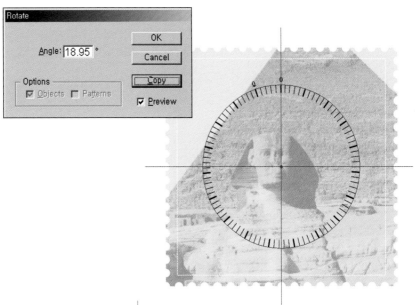

Step 10

Choose Object, Transform, Transform Again (Command/Ctrl + D) to repeat the command applied in the Rotate dialog box in Step 9. Continue to press Command/Ctrl + D to position the numbers on the darkened direction lines.

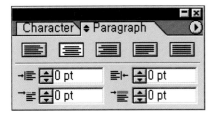

Step 11

Position the numbers entered in Step 10 directly over the darkened lines by choosing Window, Paragraph to open the Paragraph palette. Select the Align Center button.

Step 12

Select the Type tool from the toolbox. Starting at 0, enter the numbers, in 20-degree intervals, around the compass, as shown here.

Step 13

Select the Type tool again to enter the directions (North, South, East, West) inside the circle. Beneath 0, enter "NO." In the Character palette, set the Font to Times New Roman, Size to 6pt, and then press Enter.

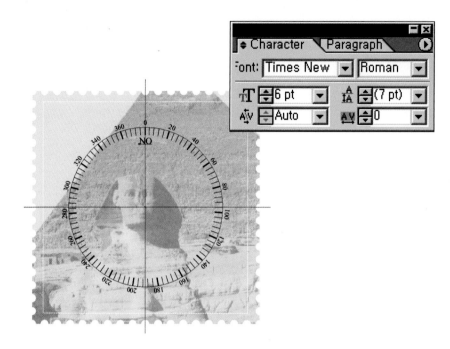

Step 14

Select the Rotate tool to copy and rotate the text 45 degrees. Hold down the Option/Alt key while clicking on the center of the stamp to open the Rotate dialog box. Set the Angle to 45° and then click the Copy button. Repeat this step by pressing Command/Ctrl + D.

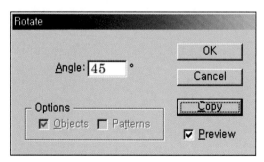

Step 15

Repeat Steps 13 and 14 to enter in the remaining directions.

ELEMENT 4
Making the Compass Needle Using the Reflect Tool

Step 1
Create a new layer in the Layers palette and name it "arrow."

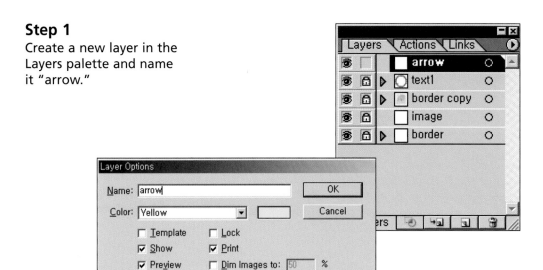

Step 2
Select the Pen tool, draw in half of the compass needle. Set the Fill Color to black and the Stroke color to None.

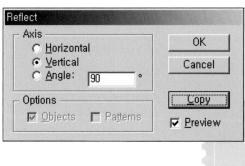

Step 3
Select the Reflect tool to draw in the other half of the compass needle. Hold down the Option/Alt key and click the center of the stamp. Select the Vertical radio button, and press the Copy button. This will create a copy of the other half of the compass needle.

Step 4

Set the Fill to white and the Stroke to black for the duplicated half of the compass needle.

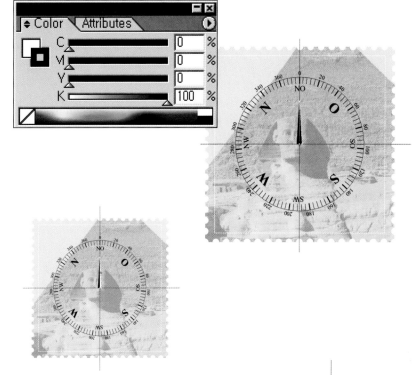

Step 5

Select both sides of the compass needle.

Step 6

Select the Rotate tool and click the center of the stamp while holding down the Option/Alt key to open the Rotate dialog box. Set the Angle to 90°, and click the Copy button. This will create a copy of the compass needle 90° from the original.

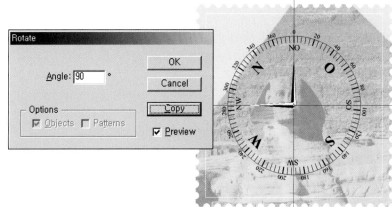

Step 7

Press Command/Ctrl + D to continue to rotate and copy the compass needle every 90°.

Step 8

Select the Ellipse tool to make the circular button at the center of the compass needle. Hold down Option/Alt + Shift to draw in a circle in the center of the stamp. Set the Fill to black.

Step 9

Repeat Step 8 to draw in another circle and set the Fill to Gradient. Select the Gradient tool to change the direction of the gradient. Draw in a smaller circle in the middle of the larger circle to add depth. Selecting the Gradient tool, click and drag a gradient in the opposite direction of the gradient at the bottom.

Step 10

You will now convert all the text into objects. Select the Selection tool and hold down the Shift key to select all the text at the same time and then choose Type, Create Outlines (Command/Ctrl + Shift + O). All of the text has now been converted to objects.

Step 11

Select the text N, O, S, W. Select Effect, Stylize, Outer Glow... from the menu bar to open the Outer Glow dialog box. Set the Mode to Screen, Opacity to 100%, Blur to 2mm, and click OK.

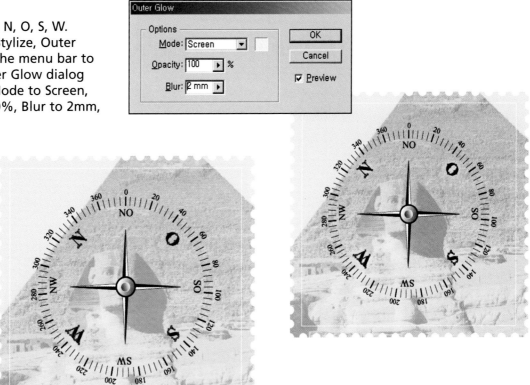

Step 12

Click an empty space in the canvas while holding down the Command/Ctrl key to exit from this function. You have now completed the compass needle.

ELEMENT 5
Completing the Time of EGYPT Souvenir Stamp

Step 1

Lock the border, image, and border copy layers. Select the compass needle made in Work 4. Reduce the size of the compass needle by double-clicking on the Scale tool to open the Scale dialog box. In the Scale dialog box, set the Uniform Scale to 92%, and click OK. The compass needle has now been reduced to 92%.

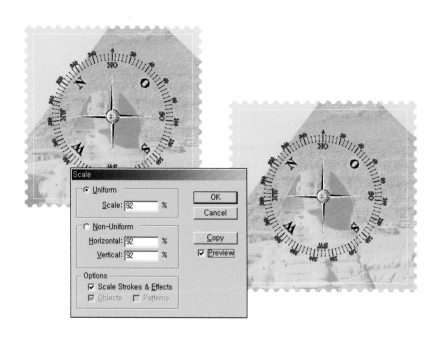

Step 2

Holding down the Command/Ctrl and Shift keys, move the compass needle up slightly.

Step 3

Selecting the Type tool, click the area where the text will be entered and type "Time of EGYPT."

Step 4

Press Command/Ctrl + T to open the Character palette and set the Font to Times New Roman, Size to 36pt, and then press Enter. Choose Type, Create Outlines to create an outline for the entered text object.

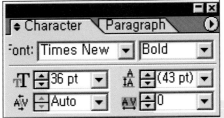

Step 5

Select the Type tool and type
"2002 EGYPT." In the Character
palette, set the Font to Freestyle
Script, the Size to 21pt, and
press Enter.

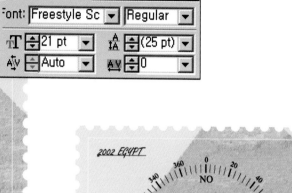

Step 6

Choose Type, Create
Outlines to create an outline
for the entered text object
(Command/Ctrl + Shift + O).
You have now completed the
Time of EGYPT stamp, part
of the Egyptian souvenir
stamp series.

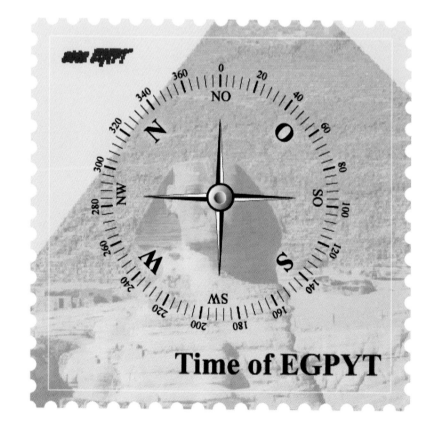

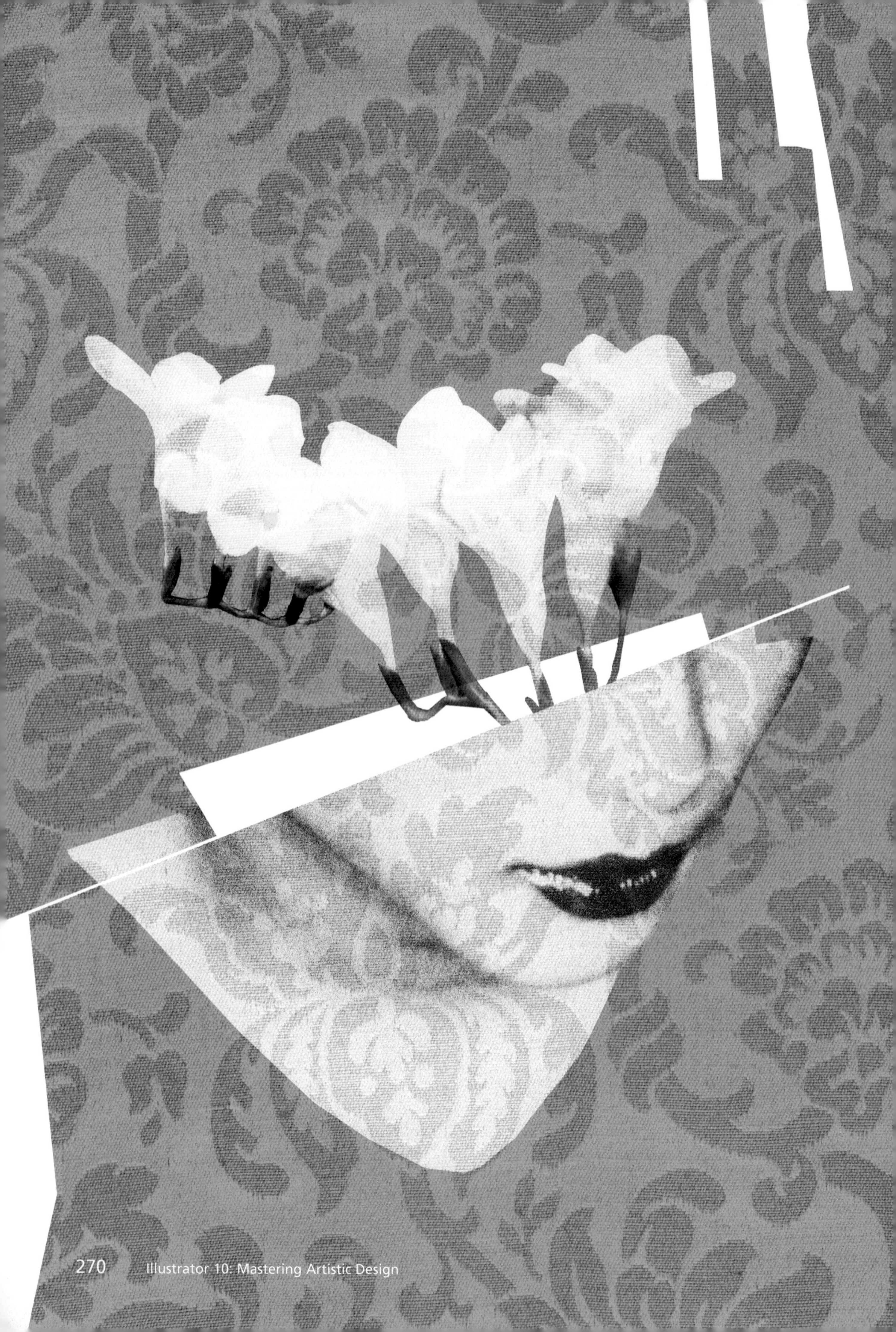

Project 8
Wallpainting of Egypt

PROJECT 8
Wallpainting of EGYPT

Illustrator 10 offers new and original type and drawing features that improve the designing process. You will use these tools to complete the simple Egyptian postage stamp design.

Source Files

Wallpainting.ai

Stamp_Border.ai

ELEMENT 1
Making the Stamp Outline Frame

Step 1

Choose File, Open from
the menu bar to open the
BOOK_10/PROJECT08/SOURCE/
STAMP _BORDER.AI file from
the supplementary CD-ROM.
You are now preparing to
make the second in our series
of Egyptian stamps, the
Wallpainting of Egypt. Choose
File, Save as, enter the name
Wallpainting of Egypt, and
click OK.

Step 2

Set the Fill to black and the
Stroke to None.

Step 3

Make the ruler visible by choosing View, Show Rulers (Command/Ctrl + R). Select the stamp border while holding down the Command/Ctrl key to show the dot in the center. Click and drag the top and left sides of the ruler to arrange them in the center of the stamp.

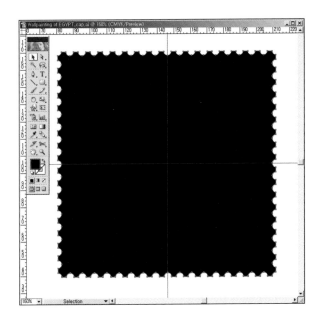

Step 4

Select the Rectangle tool from the toolbox. Click the center of the guide while pressing Option/Alt + Shift to make a rectangle. Use the Selection tool to select both objects.

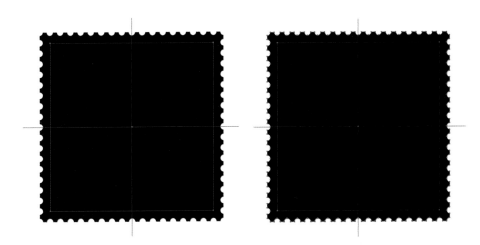

Step 5

Choose Window, Pathfinder (Shift + F9) to open the Pathfinder palette. This will allow you to make the bordering frame for the stamp. Select the Exclude overlapping shape areas button to cut out the shape on top from the shape on the bottom, as shown here.

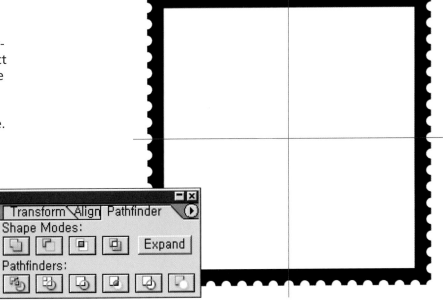

ELEMENT 2
Using the Mural to Draw the Image

Step 1

Choose File, Open to open the BOOK_10/PROJECT08/SOURCE/WALLPAINTING.AI file from the supplementary CD-ROM. This will load the image of the mural.

Step 2

Using the Selection tool, click and drag over the top portion of the image of the man on the left, which will be used in the stamp. Press Command/Ctrl + C to copy the selected image.

Step 3

Choose Window, Wallpainting of Egypt to activate this image. Create a new layer in the Layers palette and name it "image." Click the image layer to select it and drag it below the border layer.

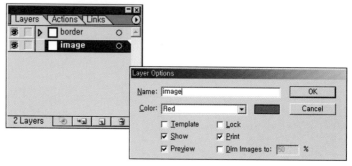

Step 4

Press Command/Ctrl + V to paste the copied image into the image layer.

Step 5

To magnify the size of the image to fit the size of the stamp, double-click the Scale tool to open the Scale dialog box. In this dialog box, set the Uniform Scale to 180%, and click OK. The Wallpainting image has been enlarged.

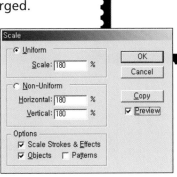

Step 6

Using the Direct Selection tool, click the portion of the skirt that extends below the stamp frame and press the Del key to remove it.

Step 7

Using the Pen tool, blend the curves to make the background as shown here. In the toolbox, select Fill and click Gradient to fill in the image with a gradient color.

Step 8

Choose Window, Gradient to open the Gradient palette. Clicking the color tab below the gradient spectrum, adjust the CMYK colors in the Color palette to create a golden yellow gradient.

Step 09
Use the Type tool to type "Wallpainting of EGYPT."

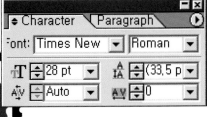

Step 10
Press Command/Ctrl + T to open the Character palette. Set the Font to Times New Roman, Size to 28pt, and press Enter. Choose Type, Create Outlines to create an outline for the entered text object (Command/Ctrl + Shift + O).

Step 11

Select the Type tool and type "2002 EGYPT." In the Character palette, set the Font to Freestyle Script, the Size to 21pt, and press Enter.

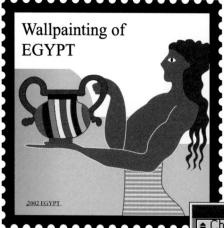

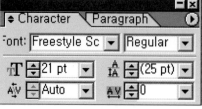

Step 12

Choose Type, Create Outlines to create an outline for the entered text object (Command/Ctrl + Shift + O). You have completed the Wallpainting of EGYPT stamp.

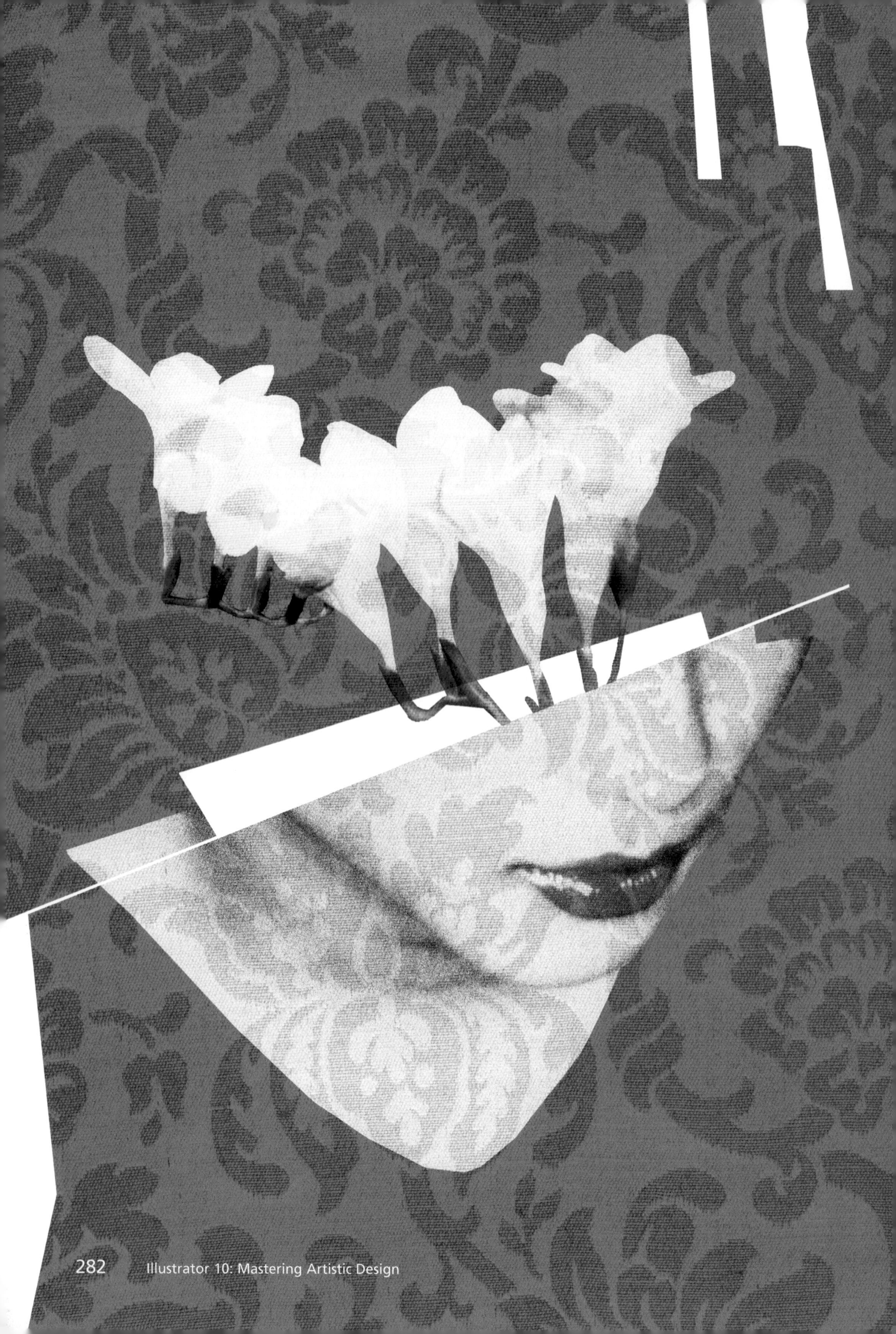

Project 9
Pyramids

PROJECT 9
Pyramids

The Clipping Mask feature is a versatile tool for cropping and filtering images. Masks provide many options for creating images. In this project, you will use the two pyramid images to complete the postage stamp.

Source Files

Stamp_Border.ai

Pyramid01.jpg

Pyramid02.jpg

ELEMENT 1
Drawing the Background for the Pyramid Stamp

Step 1

Open the BOOK_10/
PROJECT09/SOURCE/STAMP_
BORDER.AI file from the
supplementary CD-ROM. You
are now making the preparations to make the third in
our series of Egyptian stamps,
Pyramids. Choose File, Save as,
enter the File name Pyramids,
click OK.

Step 2

Set the Fill color to black and
the Stroke color to None.
Then, click an empty space on
the canvas while holding down
the Command/Ctrl key to exit
from this function.

Step 3

Create a new layer in the
Layers palette and name
it "image."

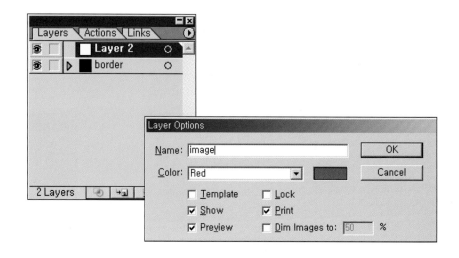

Step 4

Choose File, Place to open the BOOK_10/PROJECT09/SOURCE/ PYRAMID02.JPG file from the supplementary CD-ROM.

Step 5

Reduce the size of the image to fit the stamp by double-clicking on the Scale tool to open the Scale dialog box. In this dialog box, set the Uniform Scale to 95%, click OK.

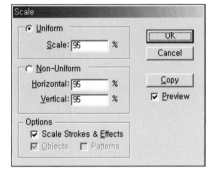

Step 6

In the Layers palette, drag and drop the border layer onto the Create New Layer icon to make the border copy layer. With the border copy layer selected, click and drag it above the image layer. This will move the black stamp border to the very top.

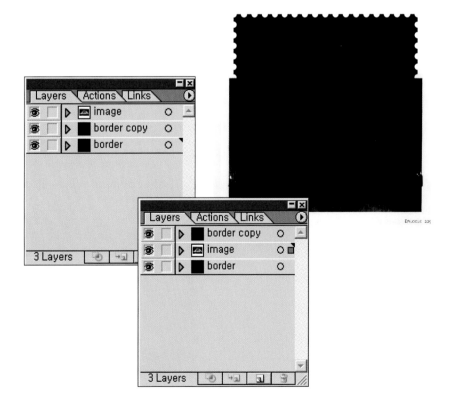

Step 7

Select all the elements of the image. To apply the mask in the shape of the topmost stamp border, choose Object, Clipping Mask, Make (Command/Ctrl + 7). Click an empty space in the canvas to exit from this function.

Step 8

Looking at the Layers palette, you can see that a Group layer has been created below the border copy layer. Select the image layer below the Group layer. The mask will be applied to all objects that are drawn in the layer.

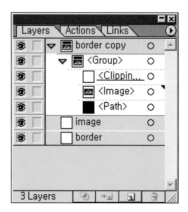

Step 9

Using the Rectangle tool, draw a rectangle to cover the white portion at the top of the image. You can see that a Path layer is created above the image layer and the mask function of the topmost layer is also applied to the rectangle.

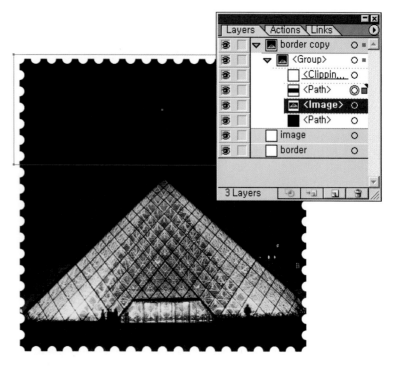

Step 10

Draw the background image in the Path layer of the Layers palette. Using the Pen tool, draw the shape seen here.

Step 11

In the Color palette, select the Fill color and adjust the CMYK slider to create a golden yellow color.

ELEMENT 2
Masking the JPG Image

Step 1
Choose File, Place to open the BOOK_10/PROJECT09/SOURCE/PYRAMID01.JPG file from the supplementary CD-ROM.

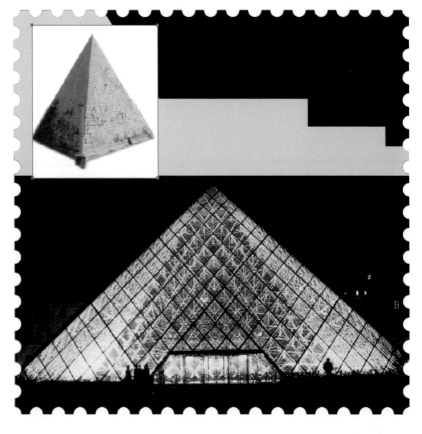

Step 2
You need to remove the white portions outside the pyramid.

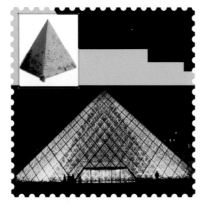

First, use the Rectangle tool to draw a rectangle the size of the pyramid image. Set both the Fill and Stroke colors to None. Use the Pen tool to draw in a pyramid on top of the image.

Step 3

Use the Selection tool to select the PYRAMID01.JPG image and the rectangular and pyramid elements drawn in Step 02. Choose Object, Clipping Mask, Make (Command/Ctrl + 7) to hide all the images in the white portion of the background, excluding the pyramid shape. Click an empty portion of the canvas to exit from this function.

ELEMENT 3
Entering Text to Complete the Pyramids Stamp

Step 1

Create a new layer and name it "image."

Step 2

Select the Type tool and type the text shown here. Open the Character palette by pressing Command/Ctrl + T and adjust the Font and Size.

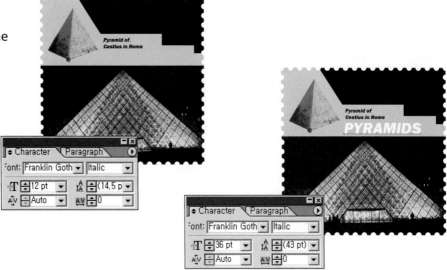

Step 3

Select the text. Choose Type, Create Outlines to create an outline for the text.

Step 4

Use the Rectangle tool to make the bordering frame for the stamp as shown here. Set the Fill to None and the Stroke to white. You have completed the pyramids stamp, one of the stamps in the Egyptian souvenir stamp series.

2002 EGYPT

Pyramid of
Cestius in Rome

PYRAMIDS

Project 10
Ancient Egyptian Museum

2002 EGYPT

In spite of its remote location, Ramses wasn't the first person with the idea of carving a holy site out of the desert rock known as the Hill of Libations.

Ancient Egyptian Museum

PROJECT 10
Ancient Egyptian Museum

Illustrator does a masterful job of integrating bitmap images from other sources with its own powerful text features and effects. In this postage stamp design, you combine type, bitmaps, and Illustrator's editing tools to create and transform the illustration.

Source Files

Stamp_Border.ai

Bronze.jpg

Column.jpg

ELEMENT 1
Drawing the Background of the Ancient Egyptian Museum

Step 1

Choose File, Open from the menu bar to open the Book_10/PROJECT10/SOURCE/STAMP_ BORDER.AI file from the supplementary CD-ROM. To make the preparations for the fourth in our series of Egyptian stamps, the Ancient Egyptian Museum, choose File, Save as, enter the File name Ancient Egyptian Museum, and click OK. Set the Fill to white and the Stroke to black. Then, holding down the Command/Ctrl key, click an empty space in the canvas to exit from this function.

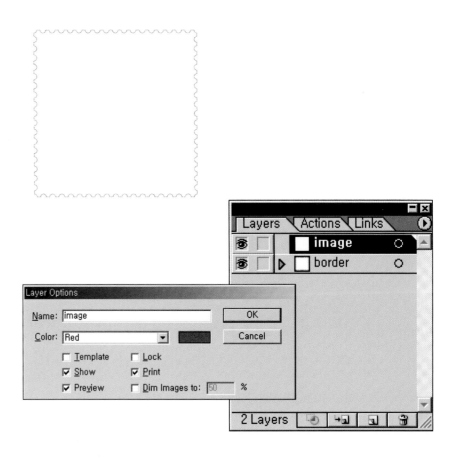

Step 2

Create a new layer in the Layers palette and name it "image."

Step 3

Choose File, Place to open the BOOK_10/PROJECT10/SOURCE/COLUMN.JPG file from the supplementary CD-ROM.

Step 4

Enlarge the size of the loaded column image to fit the stamp by double-clicking on the Scale tool to open the Scale dialog box. Set the Uniform Scale to 135%, and click OK.

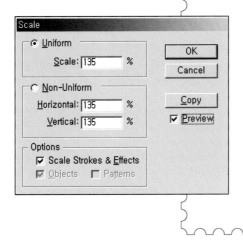

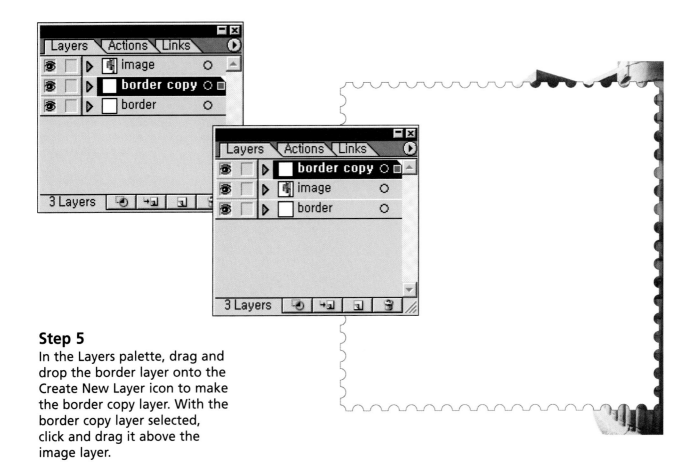

Step 5

In the Layers palette, drag and drop the border layer onto the Create New Layer icon to make the border copy layer. With the border copy layer selected, click and drag it above the image layer.

Step 6

Select all the elements of the image. Use the Clipping Mask menu to mask the image on the top layer. Choose Object, Clipping Mask, Make (Command/Ctrl + 7) to apply the mask in the shape of the stamp border. Click on an empty space in the canvas to exit from this function.

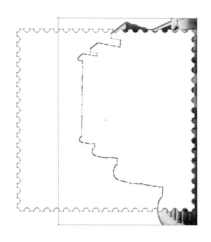

Step 7

Refer to Steps 10 and 11 in
ELEMENT 1 of PROJECT 9, use
the Pen tool to draw in the
golden yellow background at
the bottom of the image, as
shown here.

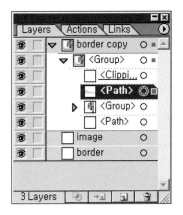

ELEMENT 2
Masking the JPG Image

Step 1

Choose File, Place to open the
BOOK_10/PROJECT10/SOURCE/
BRONZE.JPG file from the supplementary CD-ROM. Double-
click on the Scale tool to open
the Scale dialog box. Set the
Uniform Scale to 80%, and
click OK.

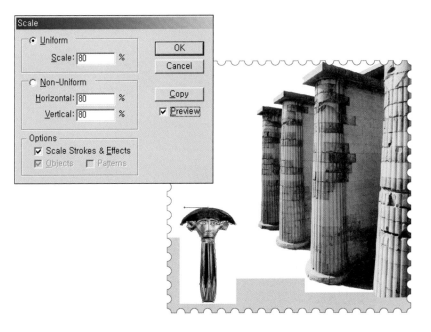

Step 2

Use the Rectangle tool to draw in a rectangle that borders the column image. Set both the Fill and Stroke colors to None. Draw in the sculpture using the Pen tool. Select the rectangle, the sculpture drawn in Step 2, and the JPG image. Choose Object, Clipping Mask, Make (Command/Ctrl + 7) to apply the mask in the shape of the stamp border. Using the Rectangle tool, draw in the rectangular frame for the stamp.

ELEMENT 3

Enter Text to Complete the Ancient Egyptian Museum Stamp

Refer to ELEMENT 3, PROJECT 9, use the Type tool to type in the text shown here. Choose Type, Create Outlines to create an outline for the text to complete the stamp (Command/Ctrl + Shift + O).

2002 EGYPT

In spite of its remote location, Ramses wasn't the first person with the idea of carving a holy site out of the desert rock known as the Hill of Libations.

Ancient
Egyptian Museum

Project 11
2002 EGYPT Souvenir Stamps

PROJECT 11
2002 EGYPT SOUVENIR STAMPS

Like Photoshop, Illustrator has a Transparency
feature. Illustrator allows you to combine Blend
modes with Opacity settings to create dynamic
effects. In this project, you will use the four postage
stamps created earlier to design a postcard. You
will manipulate the stamps and apply Shadow
effects to complete the postcard.

Source Files

Column.jpg

ELEMENT 1
Making the Background for the Stamp Series

Step 1

Open a new document (Command/Ctrl + N) and name it "Stamp_finish." In the New Document dialog box, select A4 from the Size pull-down list, set the Width to 210mm, Height to 297mm, and select the CMYK Color radio button.

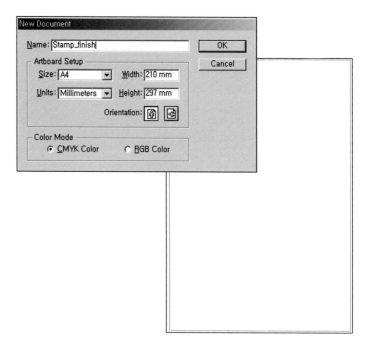

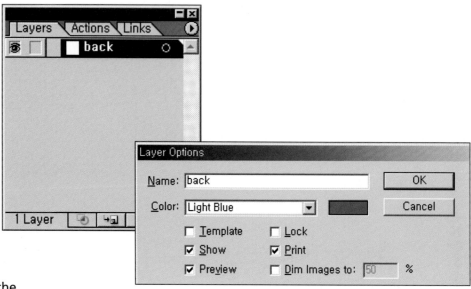

Step 2

Create a new layer from the Layers palette and name it "back." This will create the back layer, which you will use for the background.

Step 3

Select the Rectangle tool, click on the canvas to open the Rectangle dialog box. Set the Width to 120mm, Height to 160mm, and click OK. Set the Fill to a light green color.

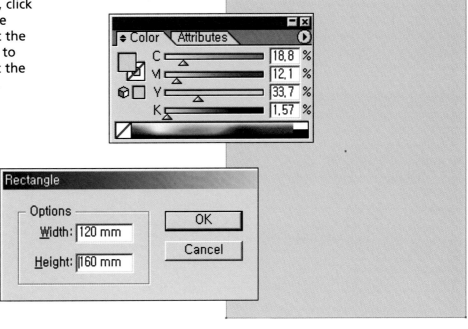

Step 4

Choose File, Place to open the BOOK_10/PROJECT11/SOURCE/ COLUMN.JPG file from the supplementary CD-ROM.

Step 5

We need to increase the size of the loaded image to fit that of the rectangle. Double-click on the Scale tool to open the Scale dialog box. Select the preview checkbox to preview the size of the image while adjusting the values. Select the image using the Selection tool and position it accordingly within the rectangle. You now need to blend the color of the background into the image. Choose Window, Transparency to open the Transparency palette. Set the Opacity to 20, and press Enter.

ELEMENT 2
Loading and Arranging the Completed Stamps

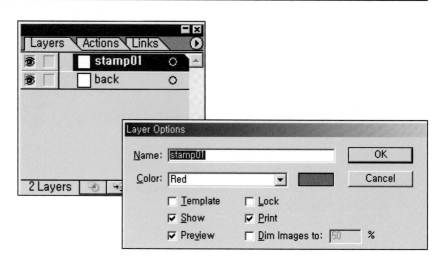

Step 1

Make a new layer in the Layers palette and name it "stamp01."

Step 2

Choose File, Open to open the BOOK_10/PROJECT11/SOURCE/STAMP01.AI file from the supplementary CD-ROM. Press Command/Ctrl + A to select the entire stamp01 image and then press Command/Ctrl + C to copy it. Choose Window, Stamp_finish and paste the copied image in the stamp01 layer. Use the Scale tool to reduce the size of the stamp. Select the stamp01 image and move it to the top left-hand corner.

Step 3

Choose File, Open to open theBOOK_10/PROJECT11/SOURCE/STAMP02, STAMP03, STAMP04.AI files from the supplementary CD-ROM using the methods described in Steps 1 and 2. Use the Scale tool to reduce the size of the stamps and use the Selection tool to position them, as shown here.

ELEMENT 3
Adding Text and Shadow Effects to the Stamps

Step 1

Select the Type tool and type "2002 EGYPT Souvenir Stamps," as shown here. Press Command/Ctrl + T to open the Character palette. Set the Font to Freestyle, Size to 36pt, and press Enter.

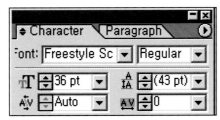

Step 2

Holding down the Command/Ctrl key, select the text, and then choose Type, Create Outlines to create an outline for the text (Command/Ctrl + Shift + O). Add shadow effects to the text by choosing Effect, Stylize, Drop Shadow. In the Drop Shadow dialog box, make the configurations shown here, and click OK.

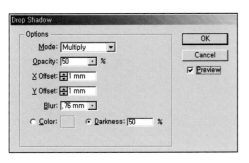

Step 3

Select the back layer in the Layers palette to make a new layer above the back layer. Select the Create New button in the Layers palette to make a new layer. Double-click on this layer to open the Layer Options dialog box and type "shadow" in the Name area.

Step 4

Lock all the layers, excluding the shadow layer, so that they are not affected by the changes to the shadow layer.

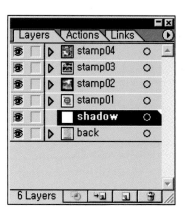

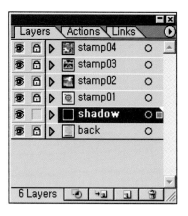

Step 5

Make the shadow by selecting the Rectangle tool and setting the Fill to black and the Stroke to None. Use the Rectangle tool to draw four rectangles below each of the four stamps where you will make the shadow.

Step 6

Click and drag the Selection tool to select each of the four rectangles.

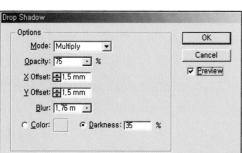

Step 7

Choose Effect, Stylize, Drop Shadow to open the Drop Shadow dialog box. Make the configurations as shown here, and click OK.

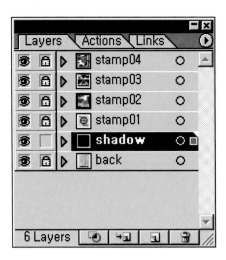

Step 8

Click on an empty space in the canvas while holding down the Command/Ctrl key to exit from this function. You have completed the Egyptian souvenir stamp series.

Project 12
Sensibility of...

PROJECT 12
Sensibility of...

In this project, you will use Illustrator's set of Liquify

tools to create a design. Liquify tools transform

images in ways that range from subtle to dramatic.

You'll also use the Twirl, Bloat, and Crystallize tools

to create a unique design.

ELEMENT 1
Making Pattern Objects

Step 1

Open a new document (Command/Ctrl + N). In the New Document dialog box type "brush" in the Name area, select A4 from the Size drop-down list, select the CMYK Color radio button, and click OK. Create a new layer in the Layers palette and name it "pattern brush."

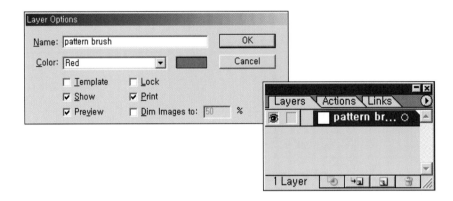

Step 2

Choose Window, Swatches to open the Swatches palette. In the Swatches palette, you can see several colors that have already been saved. You can add a color by choosing Window, Swatch Libraries, PANTONE Metallic Coated to open the PANTONE Metallic Coated color palette. Select a color and it will be added to the Swatches palette.

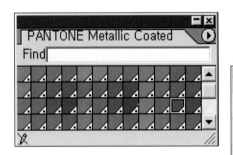

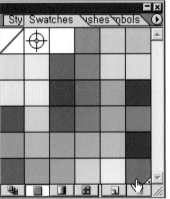

Step 3

Set the Stroke to the color shown here and use the Pen tool to draw the shape. When using the Pen tool to draw lines, it is more convenient to set the Fill to None and the Stroke to a color. After drawing the line, select the Swap Fill and Stroke button to fill in the design with the color.

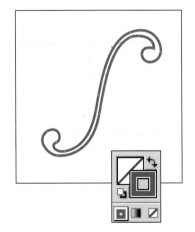

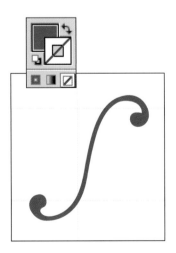

Step 4

Use the techniques described in Step 3 to draw the other designs and fill them with the same color.

Step 5

Choose Window, Pathfinder to open the Pathfinder palette (Shift + F9). Select all the elements by pressing Command/Ctrl + A, and click the Add to shape area button in the Pathfinder palette to combine the three separate elements into one.

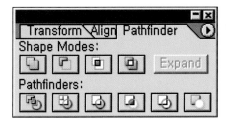

ELEMENT 2
Saving Patterns in the Swatches Palette

Step 1

Select the Show Pattern Swatches button in the Swatches palette. Use the Selection tool to select the design and drag it to the Swatches palette to save it as a swatch.

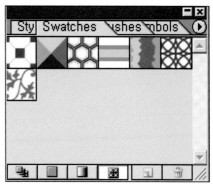

Step 2

Double-click the new pattern to open the Swatch Options dialog box. In the Swatch Options dialog box, type "bine1" in the Swatch Name area.

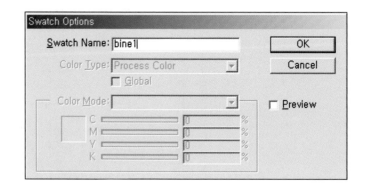

Step 3

Use the Pen tool to draw another design.

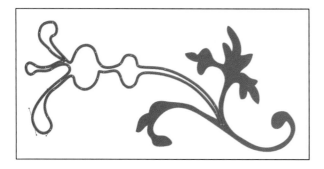

Step 4

Select the new design and click the Add to shape area button in the Pathfinder palette to combine the two separate designs into one.

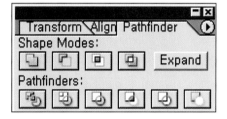

Step 5

Select the design, right-click (Command + Click) and select Transform, Reflect. In the Reflect dialog box, select the Vertical radio button, and click OK. This will make a vertically symmetrical copy of the design.

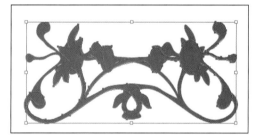

Step 6

Use the Selection tool to select the design and drag them to the Swatches palette to save the design as a swatch. Double-click the new design saved in the Swatches palette. In the Swatch Options dialog box, type "bine2" in the Swatch Name area, and click OK.

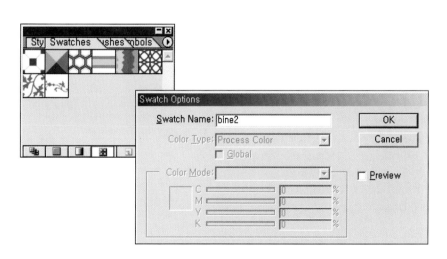

ELEMENT 3
Saving as Pattern Brushes in the Brushes Palette

Step 1

Choose Window, Brushes to open the Brushes palette (F5). Select the Option button in the Brushes palette and select New Brush. In the New Brush dialog box, choose the New Pattern Brush radio button, and click OK.

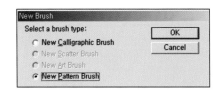

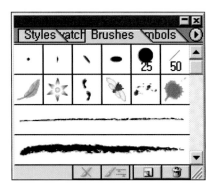

Step 2

You will now convert the two designs into pattern brushes. In the Pattern Brush Options dialog box, type "bine brush" in the Name area. Select the first area beneath Name and choose bine2 as shown here.

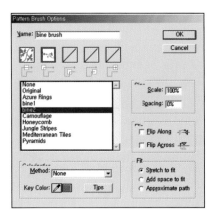

Step 3

In this project, you will apply a pattern brush to areas that are straight as well as to corners and curves. Click the outer corner tile button, select bine1, and click OK. For open figures, apply the pattern by making a pattern brush that will substitute for where the curve bends in, where the curve starts and where the curve ends.

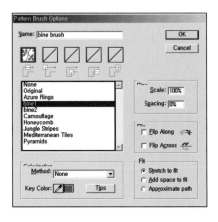

Step 4

Looking at the Brushes palette, you can see the addition of the new pattern brush.

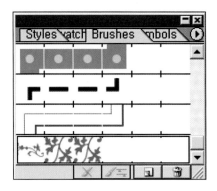

ELEMENT 4
Entering Text and Creating an Intricate Border

Step 1
Use the Type tool to adjust the Font and Size as shown here. Type in S and then, reducing the font size, type in "sensibility of..." right below it.

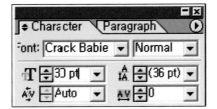
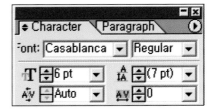

Step 2
Set the Fill to None and choose the Stroke color. Select the pattern brush that was saved in the Brushes palette. Select the Rectangle tool, hold down the Shift and Option/Alt keys to draw a square around the S. This will create a square box with the letter S in the middle.

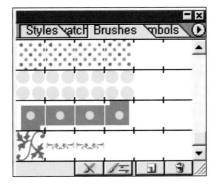

Step 3
Select the Ellipse tool, hold down the Shift and Option/Alt keys to draw a circle around the letter S.

Step 4

Draw a big ellipse initially and then reduce it to make the pattern look abundant. Use the Scale tool to reduce the size of the ellipse.

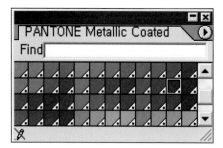

Step 5

Select the text in the middle of the pattern, choose Window, Swatches, PANTONE Process Coated. In the PANTONE Process Coated color palette, select a desired color to change the color of the text.

ELEMENT 5
Changing the Star Using the Liquify Tools

Step 1
Create a new layer and name it "background."

Step 2
Choose Window, Swatches, PANTONE Process Coated to select the fill color for the star. Apply the color from the PANTONE Solid Matte color palette. Set the Stroke color to None.

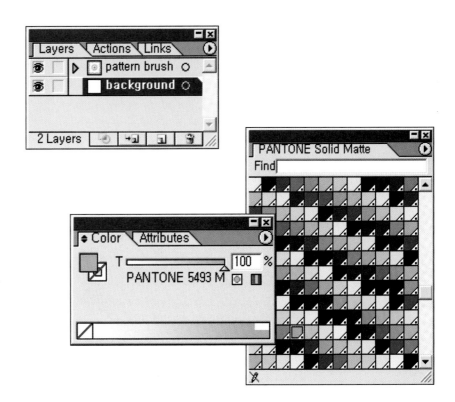

Step 3
Use the Star tool from the toolbox to draw a five-pointed star.

Step 4
Select the Twirl tool and click and drag the mouse and change the shape of the star until the desired result is achieved. The Twirl tool allows us to twirl and bend the areas on which the tool is clicked.

Step 5

Select the Bloat tool and click portions of the star to bloat the areas. Your results will not look exactly like the example here, but continue using the tool until you get the results you like. Then use the Twirl tool to approximate the look shown here.

 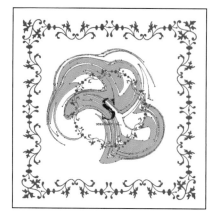

Step 6

Finally, use the Pucker tool to create the effect seen here. The Pucker tool causes the star to shrink and gather on the anchor point where it is clicked. Using the Liquify tools in this way, you can create an effect that looks like abstract art.

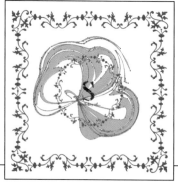

ELEMENT 6
Changing the Original Object Using Liquify Tools

Step 1

Select a color. Use the Ellipse tool to draw an ellipse in the middle of the image. Set the Opacity to 47% in the Transparency palette so that the pattern you made previously can be seen.

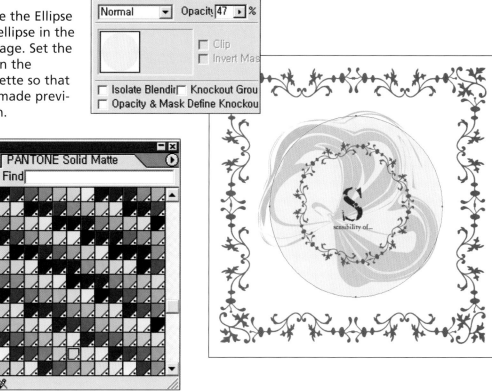

Step 2

Alter the ellipse using the Twirl and Crystallize tools to create the effect seen here.

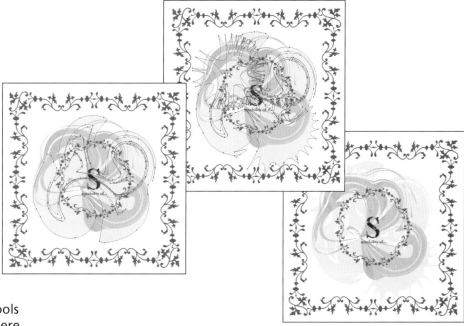

Step 3

Right-click (Command + Click) the star to select Arrange, Bring to Front (Command/Ctrl + Shift +]).

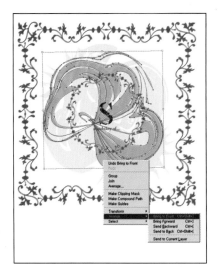

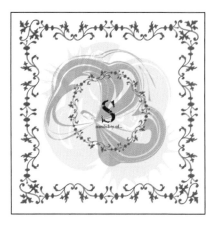

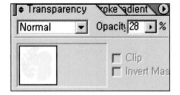

Step 4

You can see that the color of the altered star is too dark, making the text hard to see. Select each of the elements as shown, and set the Opacity to 28% and 32% in the Transparency palette. This completes the design.

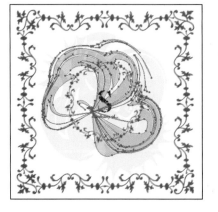

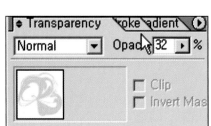

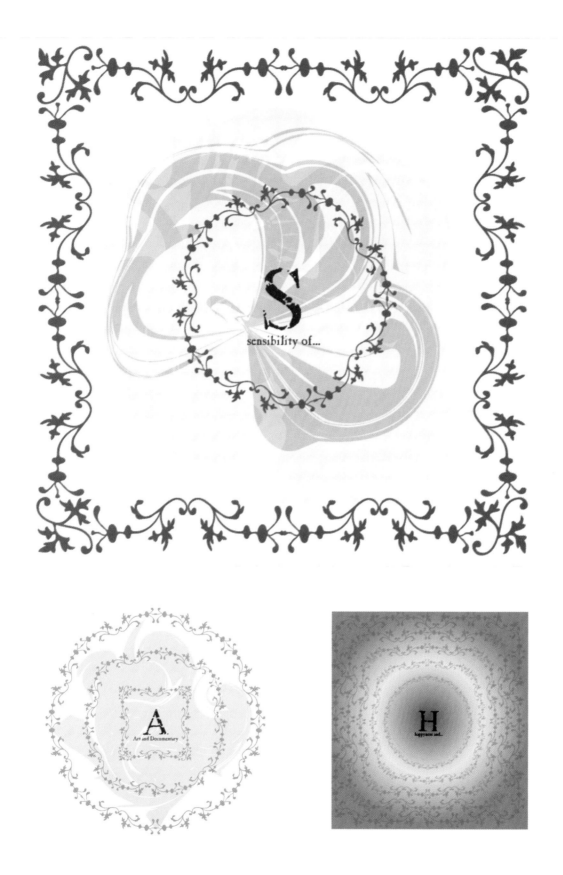

Using the Pattern Brush and other Illustrator tools, you were able to easily create this rather complex-looking pattern. Depending on how you alter the shapes, you can create totally different styles.

Project 13
City Map Design

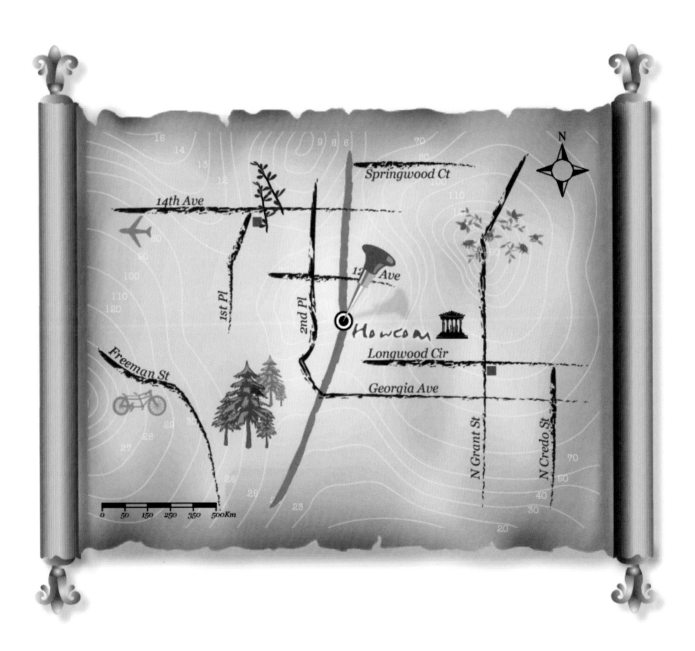

PROJECT 13
City Map Design

The Symbols palette will be used to create a distinctive, weathered-looking map. You will make symbols and save them in the Symbols palette to easily manage repeating graphics and reduce the file size. Original artwork can be stored as a symbol. Symbols make Web site management easier since you can globally update artwork by replacing symbols.

Source Files

Pin.ai

Shrine.jpg

ELEMENT 1
Making a 3D Scroll

Step 1

Open a new document (Command/Ctrl + N). In the New Document dialog box type "map" in the Name area, select A4 in the Size pull-down list, select the horizontal orientation button and the CMYK Color radio button.

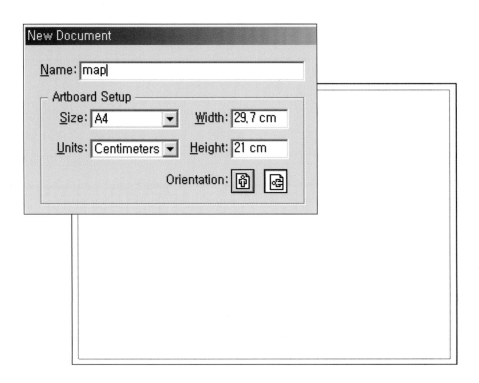

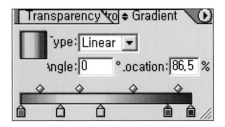

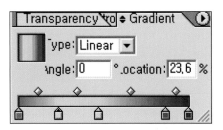

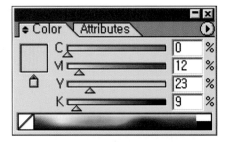

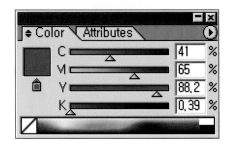

Step 2

Select the Gradient tool and set the Type to Linear in the Gradient palette. Set the color in the Color palette as shown here.

Step 3

Draw two long rectangles as shown here. Select the Gradient tool and click and drag the mouse over the rectangles until they appear rounded. Holding down the Shift key when making the gradient will create a horizontal gradient and the scope of the gradient will depend on how far you drag the mouse. Rename Layer 1 "column."

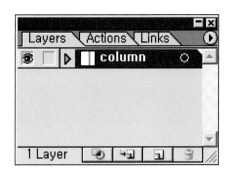

Step 4

Set the Stroke to a dark blue color. Using the Line Segment tool, draw in a vertically straight line on the right end of the rounded object. Click and drag on this line segment while holding down the Shift key to make a copy on the left side. Set the Stroke to a sky blue color. Again, make a copy of the line segment on the left side and then change the color to a dark blue again to complete the line segment.

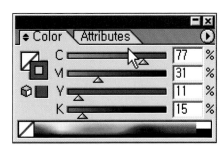

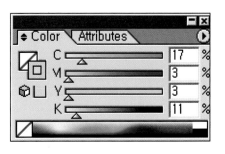

Step 5

Select the two line segments as shown here. Choose Object, Blend, Blend Options to open the Blending Options dialog box and set the Spacing to Specified Steps and enter 8. Select the Blend tool from the toolbox, click once on the right and left anchor points. This will blend the selected line segments. Blend the remaining line segments in the same way.

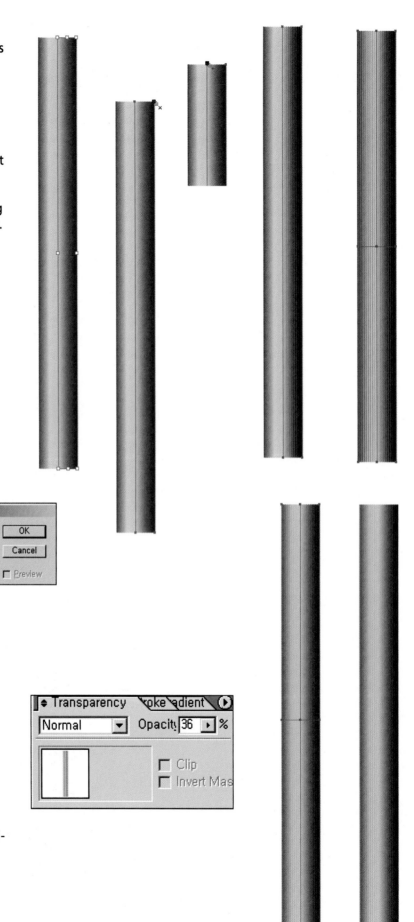

Step 6

You can see that the blend color is too dark and the gradient is hard to see. So, set the Opacity to 36% in the Transparency palette.

ELEMENT 2
Making 3D Decorative Objects

Step 1

Use the Rounded Rectangle tool to draw in a rounded rectangle. Select the Gradient button to fill in the rectangle with the gradient color. Drag the Color tab in the Gradient palette outside the palette to remove unnecessary tabs.

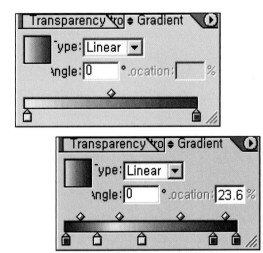

Step 2

Select the rounded rectangle and right-click the mouse to select Arrange, Send to Back (Command/Ctrl + Shift + [). Use the Rectangle tool to draw a rectangle on top of the rounded rectangle.

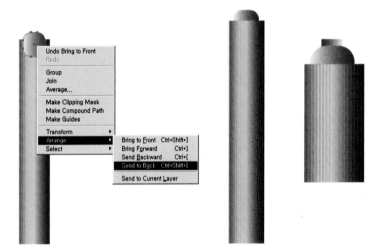

Step 3

Use the Pen tool to draw in the remaining objects and then apply the gradient to add depth. In the Gradient palette, set the Type to Radial and Linear to apply the gradient evenly throughout the object.

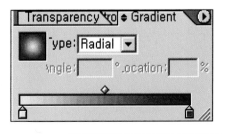

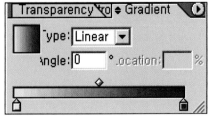

Step 4

Select all the decorative elements using the Selection tool, group them together by choosing Object, Group (Command/Ctrl + G). Right-click the mouse and select Transform, Reflect. In the Reflect dialog box, select the Horizontal checkbox and click Copy. A copy of the mirror reflection of the element will be made against the vertical axis. Select the duplicated element while holding down the Shift key and move it to the bottom.

Step 5

Select all the elements by choosing Select, All (Command/Ctrl + A). Then, lock the elements by choosing Object, Lock, Selection (Command/Ctrl + 2).

Step 6

Using the Pen tool, draw the irregular mask objects as shown here to create the effect of old paper. Set the Fill to None.

Step 7

Unlock the selected objects by choosing Object, Unlock All (Command/Ctrl + Option/Alt + 2). Use the Selection tool to select the rounded rectangle and the mask object. Then, choose Object, Clipping Mask, Make (Command/Ctrl + 7). You can see that the shape of the mask object has changed. When doing this, you must make sure that the mask object is arranged on the very top of the selected objects.

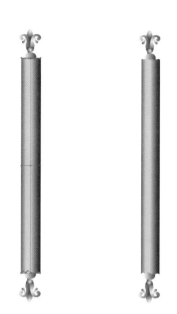

ELEMENT 3
Making Faded Paper Objects

Step 1

Create a new layer and name it "paper."

Step 2

Set the Stroke to None and the Fill to yellow. Draw the rectangle seen here.

Step 3

Choose Object, Create Gradient Mesh. In the Create Gradient Mesh dialog box, select the Preview checkbox, and click OK.

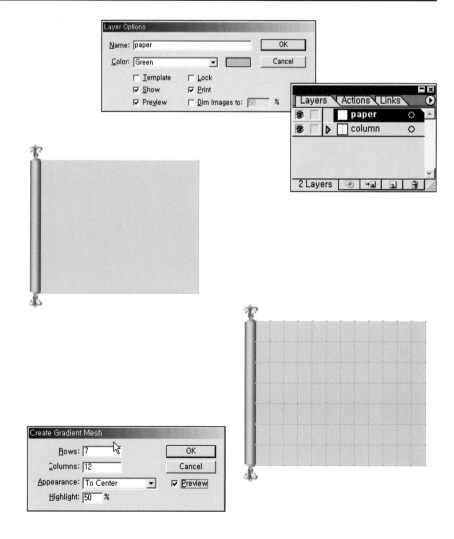

Step 4

Select the Mesh tool, select one of the mesh points. This will activate the editable form of the mesh point by creating directional lines. Select a color appropriate for the mesh point.

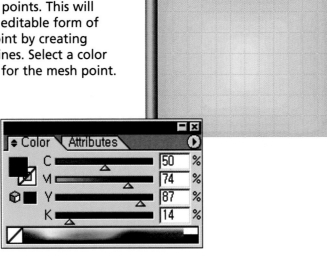

Step 5

Repeating Step 04, click on the mesh points and select the appropriate color in the Color palette to add shading to the paper.

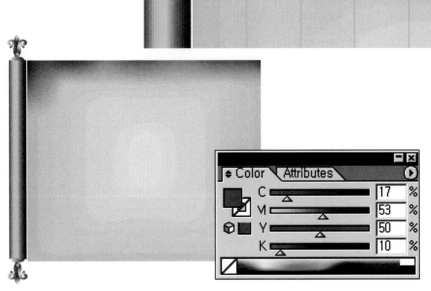

Step 6

Moving the mouse to the mesh line rather than the mesh point will change the mouse cursor to a +. Clicking the mouse at this time will add a mesh line. Conversely, to remove a mesh line, click on a mesh point while holding down the Option/Alt key.

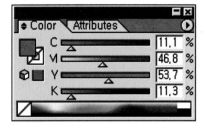

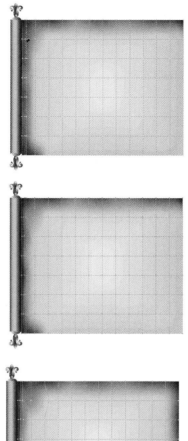

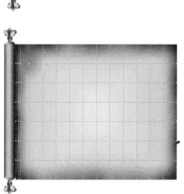

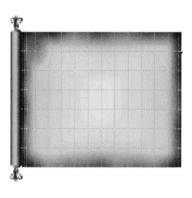

Step 7

Repeat this process to complete the gradient mesh.

ELEMENT 4

Applying Masks to Create the Effect of Ripped Paper

Step 1

Lock the column layer.

Step 2

Create the effect of old paper by using the Pen tool to draw in the irregular mask objects shown here. Set the Fill to None and Stroke to the color shown.

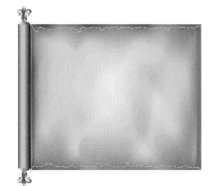

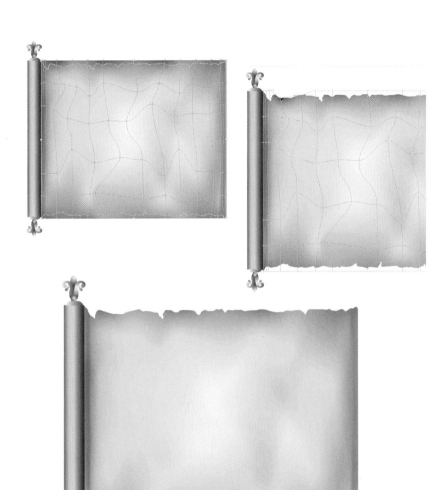

Step 3

Select the rectangle to which the gradient mesh has been applied, and the mask object. Then, choose Object, Clipping Mask, Make (Command/Ctrl + 7). You can see that the shape of the rectangle has changed to that of the mask object.

Step 4

Unlock all the layers by choosing Object, Unlock All (Command/Ctrl + Option/Alt + 2). Select the column and right-click the mouse to select Transform, Reflect.

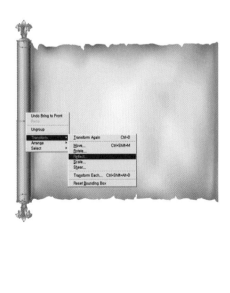

Step 5

In the Reflect dialog box, select the Vertical radio button and click Copy. Drag the copied object to the right while holding down the Shift key. Holding down the Shift key allows us to move the objects horizontally or vertically.

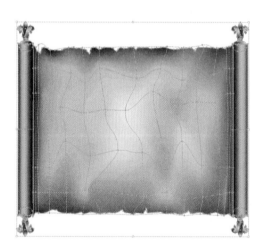

Step 6

Select all the objects by choosing Select, All (Command/Ctrl + A). Choose Effect, Stylize, Feather and in the Feather dialog box, set the Radius to 2px. The Feather value will be applied to the selected object to soften the edges like a bitmap image.

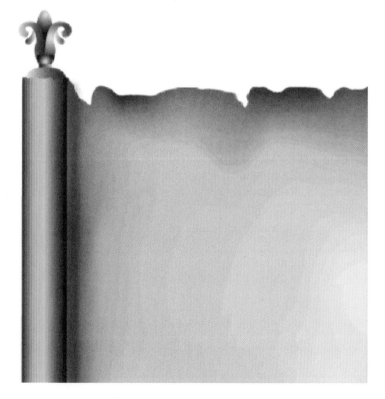

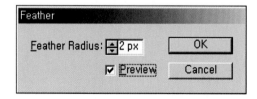

ELEMENT 5
Adding Shadow Effects to Complete the Scroll

Step 1
Using the Selection tool to select the rectangular paper object, choose Effect, Stylize, Drop Shadow. In the Drop Shadow dialog box, enter the values shown here, and click OK.

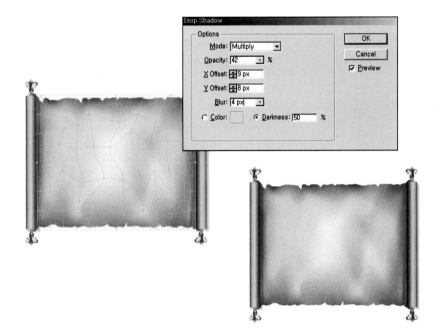

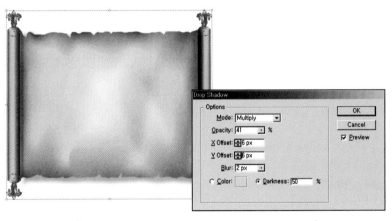

Step 2
Select the decorative objects. Choose Effect, Stylize, Drop Shadow. In the Drop Shadow dialog box, enter the values shown here, and click OK.

Step 3

In the same way, select the columns and apply shadow effects. Adding the shadow effects completes the making of the faded scroll.

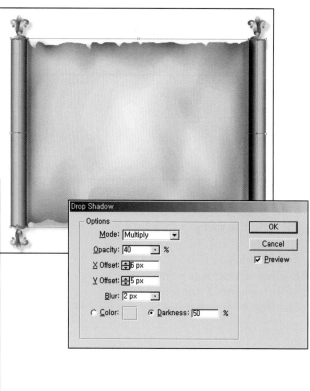

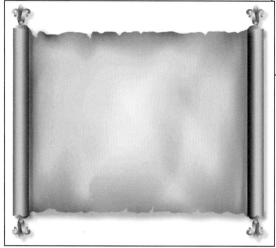

ELEMENT 6
Making Contour Lines I

Step 1

Create a new layer and name it "contour line." Lock all the other layers.

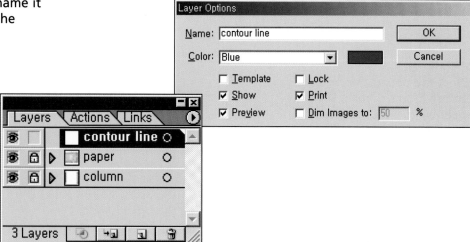

Step 2

In the Color palette, set the Fill to None and establish the Stroke color. Using the Pen tool, draw the small contour line shown here and then draw a slightly larger one around it.

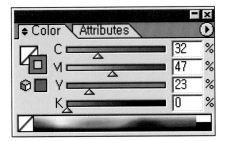

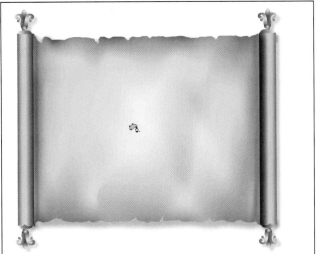

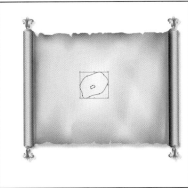

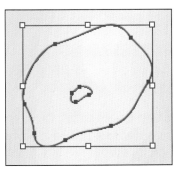

Step 3

Use the Selection tool to select both contour lines and then double-click on the Blend tool to open the Blend Options dialog box. In the Blend Options dialog box, set the Spacing to Specified Steps and enter 5. Then, choose Object, Blend, Make to apply blend to the selected objects. (Command/Ctrl + Option/Alt + B).

Step 4

Use the Pen tool to draw the same two contour lines you drew in the previous step on the right-hand side of the scroll. Double-click on the Blend tool to open the Blend Options dialog box. In the Blend Options dialog box, set the Spacing to Specified Steps and enter 3. Then, choose Object, Blend, Make to apply blend to the selected objects (Command/Ctrl + Option/Alt + B).

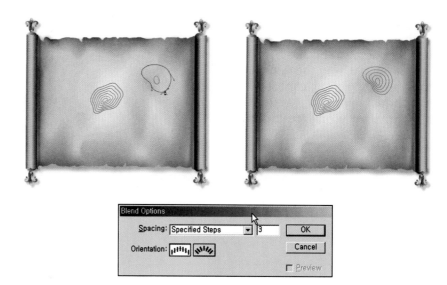

Step 5

Use the Pen tool to draw the large contour line shown here. Double-click on the Blend tool to open the Blend Options dialog box. In the Blend Options dialog box, set the Spacing to Specified Steps and enter 5. Then, choose Object, Blend, Make to apply blend to the selected objects (Command/Ctrl + Option/Alt + B).

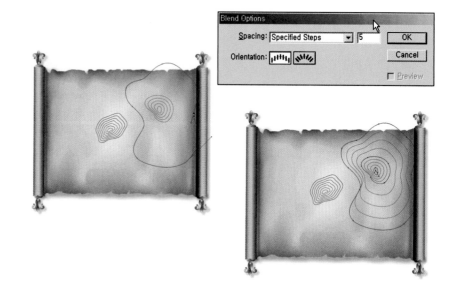

Step 6

In order to edit lines to which the Blend has already been applied, use the Direct Selection tool to click and drag on the anchor point you wish to edit until the desired result is achieved.

Step 7

Select the contour lines and drag them while holding down the Option/Alt key to copy. Double-click on the Scale tool to open the Scale dialog box. In the Scale dialog box, set the Scale to 130% to magnify the duplicated object. Rotate the object using the Rotate tool and arrange it in place.

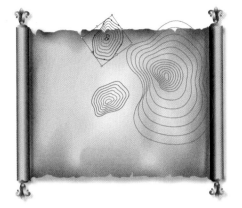

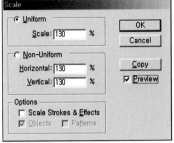

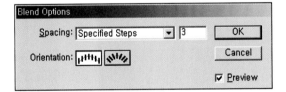

Step 8

With the duplicated object selected, double-click on the Blend tool to open the Blend Options dialog box. In the Blend Options dialog box, set the Spacing to Specified Steps and enter 3. The blended object will change according to the entered value.

Step 9
Use the Pen tool to draw in the lines, apply Blend to complete the contour lines.

ELEMENT 7
Making Contour Lines II

Step 1
Select all the contour lines. In the Transparency palette, set the Blending Mode to Color Dodge and the Opacity to 31%.

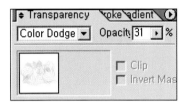

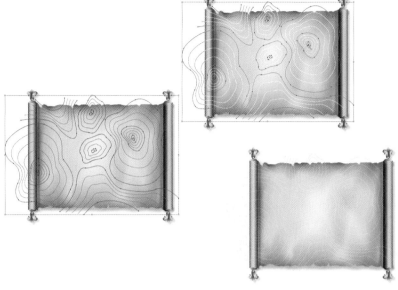

Step 2
Use masks to remove the portions of the contour lines that extend beyond the edges of the scroll. Use the Rectangle tool to draw a rectangle the size of the scroll paper. Select the contour lines and the rectangle. Choose Object, Clipping Mask, Make to apply the mask (Command/Ctrl + 7).

Step 3
Select the Type tool and press Command/Ctrl + T to open the Character dialog box. In the Character dialog box, enter the values for the Font and Size shown here.

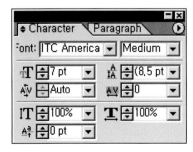

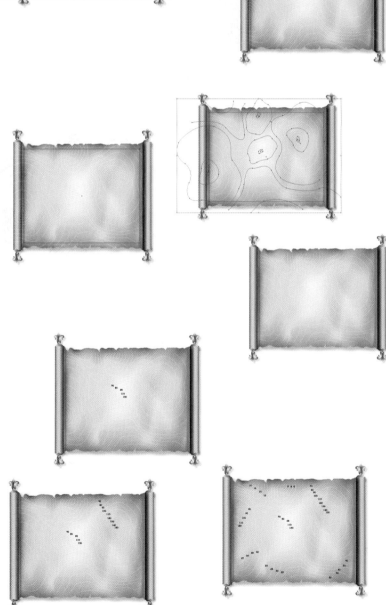

Step 4

Select the contour lines, temporarily lock the selected objects by choosing Object, Lock, Selection (Command/Ctrl + 2).

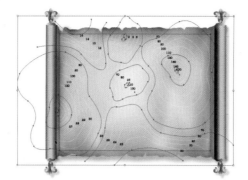 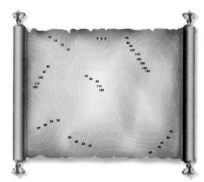

Step 5

Drag the Selection tool over the entered numbers to select them. Set the Fill to white.

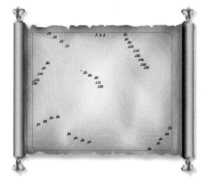 

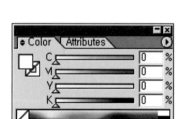

Step 6

In the Transparency palette, set the Blending Mode to Soft Light and the Opacity to 100%. This will create soft contour lines.

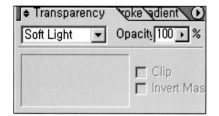

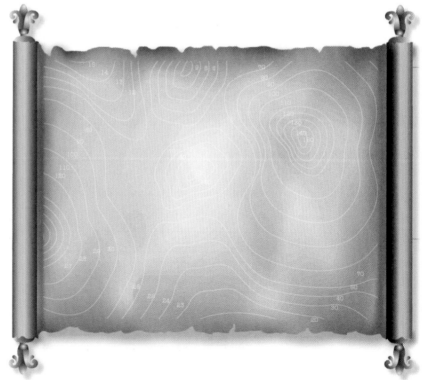

ELEMENT 8
Drawing Artistic Map Lines

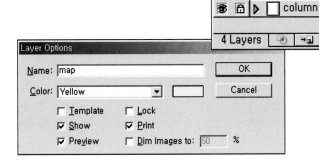

Step 1

Create a new layer and name it "map." Lock the contour line layer.

Step 2

Draw the lines shown here using the Pen tool.

Step 3

Use the Selection tool to select all the lines, excluding the line in the middle. Select the Stroke in the Color palette and click on Art Brush in the Brushes palette to apply brush effect to the selected line.

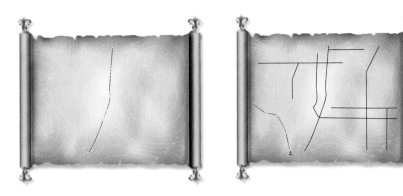

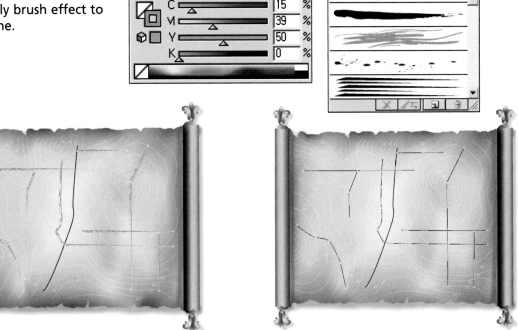

Step 4

Select the line in the middle. Select the Stroke and click on Art Brush in the Brushes palette to apply brush effect to the selected line. The thickness of the brush stroke can be adjusted in the Stroke palette. In the Stroke palette, set the Weight to 0.75.

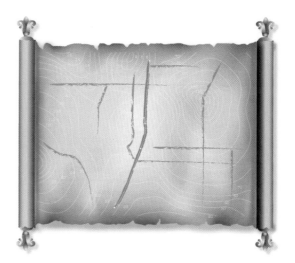

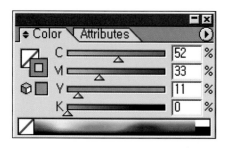

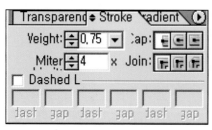

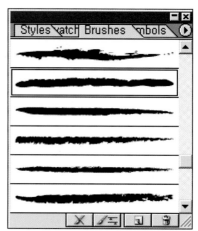

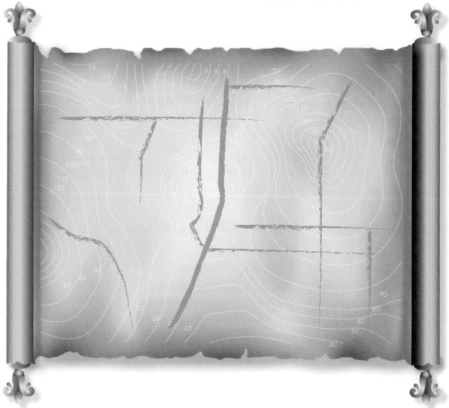

ELEMENT 9
Entering Place Names

Step 1
Select the map lines on the bottom left. Copy the objects by choosing Edit, Copy (Command/Ctrl + C). Paste the copied objects in front of the selected object by selecting Edit, Paste in Front (Command/Ctrl + F). The object is pasted perfectly in front of the selected object.

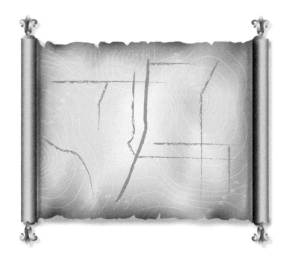

Step 2
Select the Type tool and press Command/Ctrl + T to open the Character palette. Adjust the Font and Size in the Character palette. Clicking the mouse on the duplicated map line will reveal an I-Beam text cursor in the direction of the line. You can type in text at the blinking cursor.

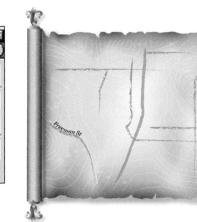

Step 3
Set the Fill color as shown here.

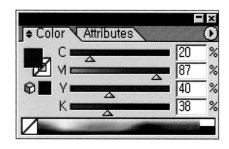

Step 4

Repeat this process to enter the rest of the place names on the map. Select all the text and then click the Eyedropper tool on the text to which the color has been applied to change the color of the selected text.

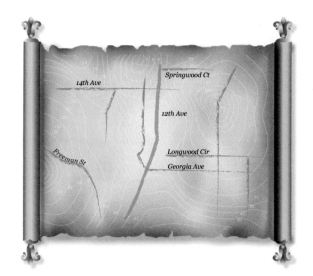

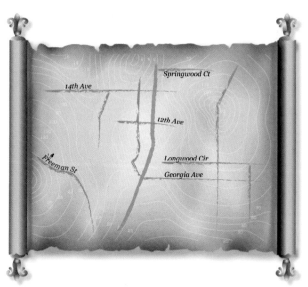

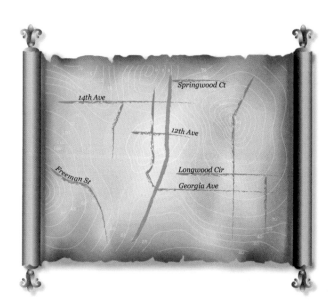

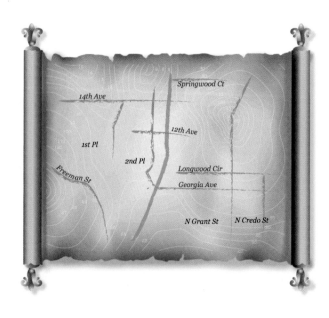

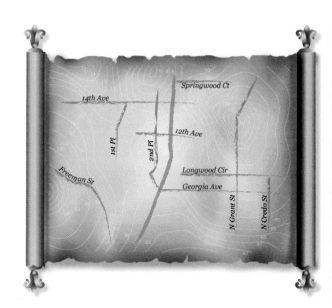

Step 5

Enter the text and then use the Rotate tool to rotate the text vertically. Select the vertically aligned text and change the color by clicking the Eyedropper tool on the text to which the color has already been applied.

Step 6

You can see that the map lines are too light, making them hard to see. Select all the map lines, excluding the blue one, and select a darker color in the Color palette.

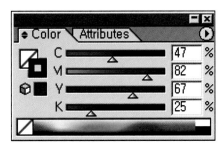
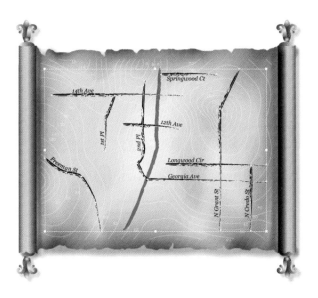

Step 7

Change the blue map line's color to green.

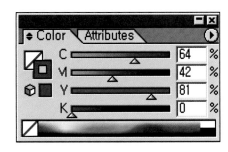
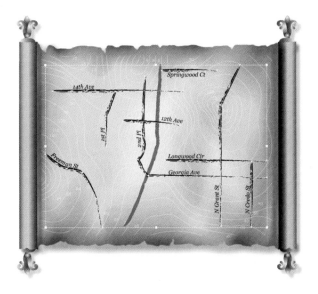

ELEMENT 10
Using Symbols to Make an Interactive Map

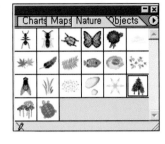
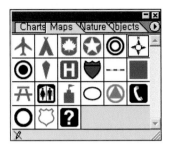

Step 1
Choose Window, Symbols to open the Symbols palette (Shift + F11). Load all symbols that are related to maps by selecting Window, Symbol Libraries, Maps.

Step 2
Select the Trees1 symbol in the Symbols palette and arrange it on the map as shown here. Reduce the size of the tree using the Scale tool. In the Transparency palette, set the Blending Mode to Luminosity and the Opacity to 52%.

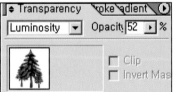

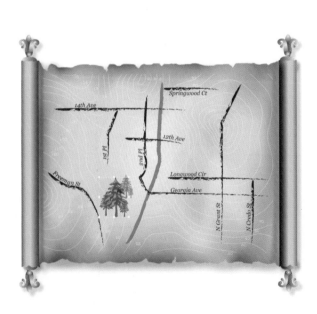

Step 3

Select the Trees1 symbol in the Symbols palette and arrange another tree on the map as shown here. In the Transparency palette, set the Blending Mode to Luminosity and the Opacity to 71%.

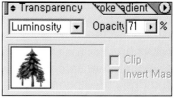

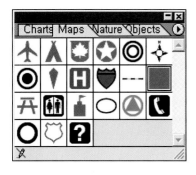

Step 4

Select and arrange the symbols shown here on the map. Making the object and saving it as a symbol will make it easier to select and use the symbol, without having to copy it and make it again, and will also reduce the file size.

Step 5

Select the Airport symbol from the Symbols palette and arrange it on the top, left-hand corner of the map. In the Transparency palette, set the Blending Mode to Exclusion and the Opacity to 36%.

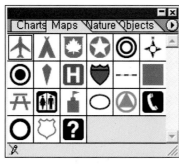

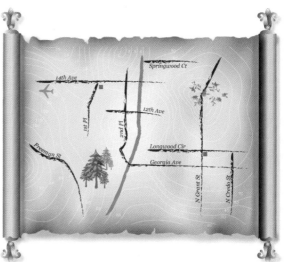

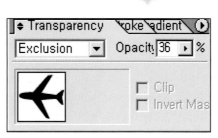

Step 6

You can also select objects from the Brushes palette and register and use them as symbols. Select Window, Brush Libraries, Other Library to select brushes that have been saved in other folders. Or, you can draw the image of the bicycle or save picture images as symbols. Drag the picture of the bicycle to the Symbols palette to save and then arrange the Bicycle symbol on the map.

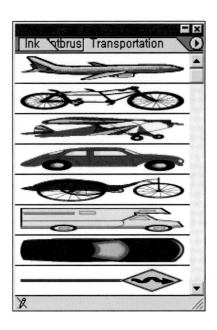

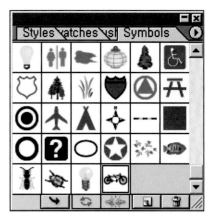

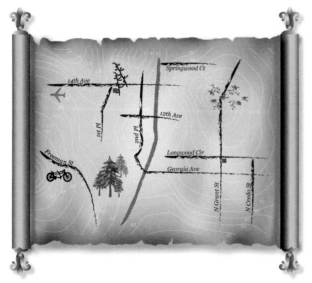

Step 7

In the Transparency palette, set the Blending Mode to Exclusion and the Opacity to 32%. This creates a more natural color for the bicycle symbol.

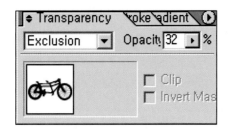

Step 8

Select the Map scale symbol from the Symbols palette and arrange it on the bottom, left-hand corner of the map. Select the Type tool and adjust the Font and Size in the Character palette. Enter the numbers below the map scale.

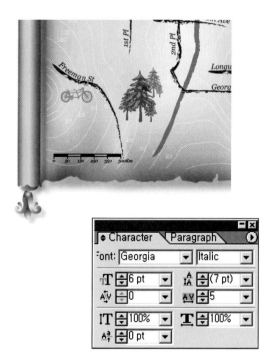

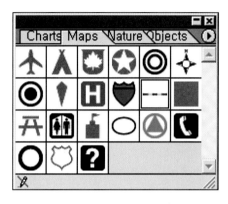

Step 9

Select the Compass rose symbol from the Symbols palette and arrange it on the top right-hand corner of the map.

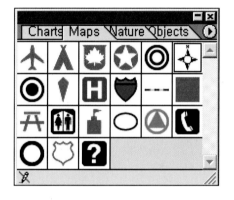

Step 10

Select Window, Brush Libraries, Other Library to select the Leaves brush, which has been saved in another folder. Drag the Leaves brush to the Symbols palette to save and then arrange the Leaves symbol on the map.

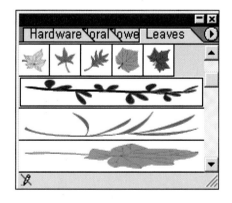

ELEMENT 11
Using Various Effects to Complete the Map

Step 1

Select the BOOK_10/PROJECT13/ SOURCE/SHRINE.JPG file from the supplementary CD-ROM and place the image in the canvas. Reduce the size of the coliseum and arrange it on the map as shown here.

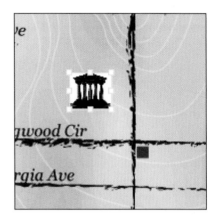

Step 2

In the Transparency palette, set the Blending Mode to Multiply and the Opacity to 74%. Because the white color is not visible, you do not need to make a separate clipping mask.

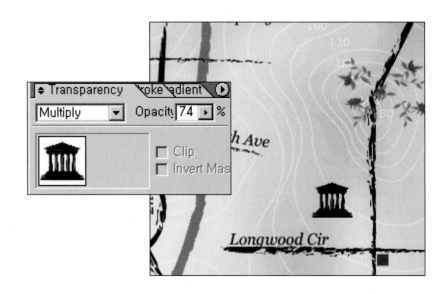

Step 3

Select the County seat symbol from the Symbols palette and arrange it in the middle of the green line.

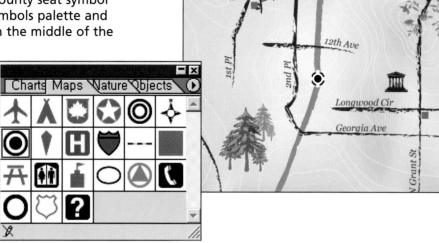

Step 4

Select the BOOK_10/PRO-JECT13/SOURCE/PIN.AI file from the supplementary CD-ROM and drag it to the Symbols palette to save.

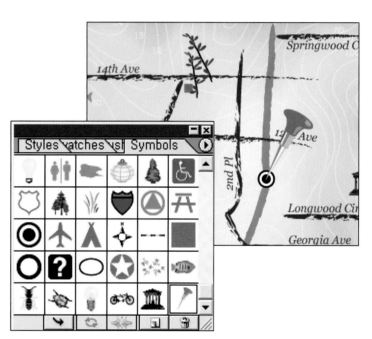

Step 5

You will now make a shadow of the pin object. Drag the pin object while holding down the Option/Alt key to make a copy. In the Transparency palette, set the Blending Mode to Difference and the Opacity to 6%. Then use the Free Transform tool to rotate and arrange the shadow of the pin object.

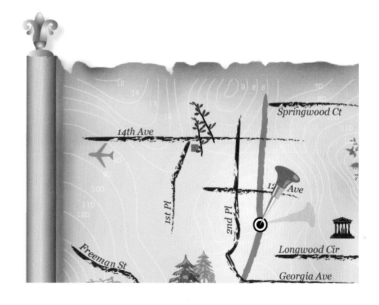

Step 6

Choose Effect, Blur, Gaussian Blur. In the Gaussian Blur dialog box, set the Radius to 2.0 pixels, and click OK to apply it to the shadow object.

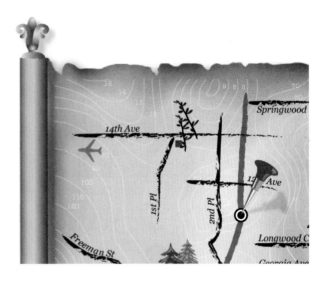

Step 7

Use the Type tool to type "Howcom." Change the color of the text to red.

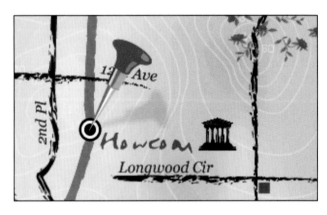

Step 8

Choose Effect, Stylize, Outer Glow. In the Outer Glow dialog box, make the configurations shown here and click OK. In order to undo effects or filters that have been applied, drag the respective effect or filter to the Delete Selected Item button in the Appearance palette.

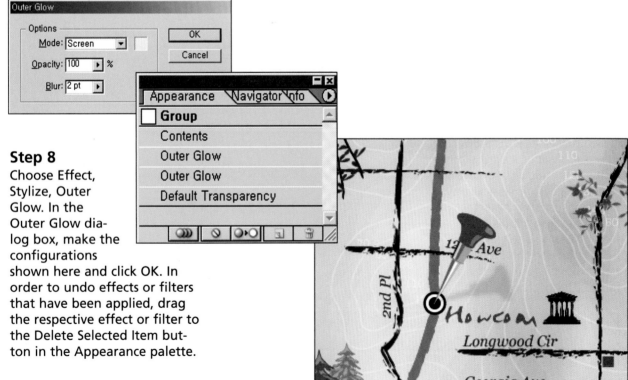

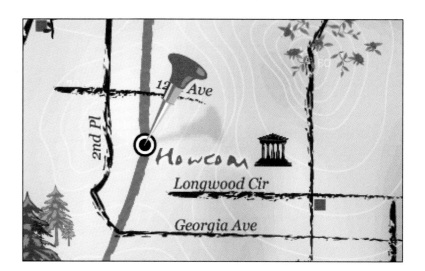

Step 9

The glow effect that has been applied to the text is difficult to see. Choose Effect, Stylize, Outer Glow to apply the Outer Glow again.

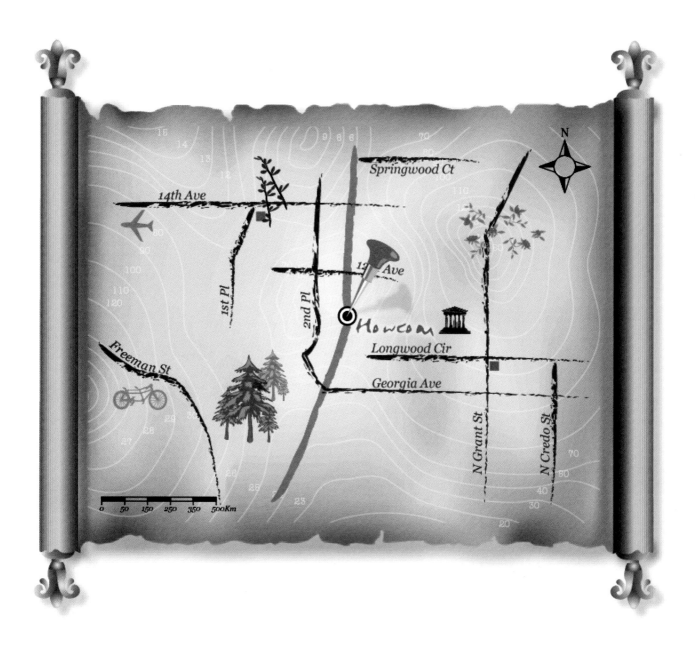